TALKING POETICS FROM
NAROPA INSTITUTE

VOLUME TWO

ANNALS OF THE
JACK KEROUAC SCHOOL
OF DISEMBODIED POETICS

Talking Poetics from Naropa Institute

VOLUME TWO

Edited by Anne Waldman and Marilyn Webb

Introduction by Allen Ginsberg

SHAMBHALA
Boulder & London
1979

SHAMBHALA PUBLICATIONS, INC.
1123 Spruce Street
Boulder, Colorado 80302

Distributed in the United States by Random House
and in Canada by Random House of Canada Ltd.
Distributed in the Commonwealth by Routledge & Kegan Paul Ltd.,
London and Henley-on-Thames.

LIBRARY OF CONGRESS CATALOGING IN PUBLICATION DATA

Main entry under title:

Talking Poetics from Naropa Institute.
    Based on lectures given at the Jack Kerouac School of
Disembodied Poetics at Naropa Institute, 1974-1977.
    Bibliography: p.
    1. Poetics—Addresses, essays, lectures. I. Waldman, Anne, 1945-
II. Webb, Marilyn. III. Naropa Institute.
    IV. Jack Kerouac School of Disembodied Poetics.
PN1042.T27   808.1   77-90884
        ISBN 0-394-73691-5 (v. 2) (Random House)

Printed in the United States.

Acknowledgements

The four parts of *Empty Words with Relevant Material*, by John Cage, have been previously published in four places: 1) in *Active Anthology*, edited by George Quasha (Fremont, Michigan: Sumac Press, 1974); 2) in *Interstate 2*, edited by Carl D. Clark and Loris Essary (Austin, Texas: 1974); 3) in *big deal 3*, edited by Barbara Baracks, 1975; and 4) in *WCH WAY*, edited by Jed Rasula (Dover, New Hampshire: 1975). Each appearance of the piece has an introduction.

"Empty Words: John Cage Talks Back," from *Loka: A Journal from Naropa Institute*, edited by Rick Fields. Copyright © 1975 by Nalanda Foundation/Naropa Institute. Reprinted by permission of Doubleday & Company, Inc.

The Content of History Will Be Poetry, by Ed Sanders, has been previously published in his book *Investigative Poetry* (San Francisco: City Lights, 1976), pp. 1-16. This work was reprinted by kind permission of the author.

A version of the talk *Poetry and Politics*, by Lewis MacAdams, was presented by the author at Bob Perelman's 1220 Folsoms "Loft-Talk" Series, on June 30, 1977, in San Francisco.

With kind permission of the publisher, Jerome Rothenberg, in his piece *Changing the Past, Changing the Present: A New Poetics*, has used excerpts from *The Cantos of Ezra Pound*, Ezra Pound (New York: New Directions, 1970). Copyright © 1940 Ezra Pound.

Permission to quote "12 Songs to Welcome the Society of the Mystic Animals," from *Shaking the Pumpkin*, edited by Jerome Rothenberg, granted by Doubleday & Company, Inc. Copyright © 1972 by Jerome Rothenberg.

TABLE OF CONTENTS

VOLUME ONE

VOLUME TWO

Photo by John Barkin

Michael Brownstein

IMAGINATION FOR ADULTS

AUGUST 19, 1975

> Any view of things that
> isn't strange is false.
>
> —Paul Valery

I WOULD LIKE to discuss imagination—that is, imaginative activity—from two related points of view: its function in various cultural contexts, and its function within individual personality—how do poets or artists see themselves? What is the value or imagery they attach to what they do?

Essentially, my interest arises from the curious and vast difference I've noticed concerning values attached to imaginative activity by primitive cultures, as opposed to the way most "civilized" people view its products. The body of myths handed down to us from primitive or tribal cultures certainly shares a point of origin with more contemporary stories, fables, improvisations and fantasy, but it is also true that modern pejorative definitions of the word "myth" as "fabrication" or "falsehood" cancel out almost all value we might receive from these stories.

This definition sees myth as "unproven assertion" rather than as participation in what is mysteriously beyond the senses. By disapproving of any assertions except those confirmed by testing of hypotheses, this attitude has relegated to the back burner of "myth" anything that is not science. As Stephen Larsen writes in *The Shaman's Doorway,* "Most of us have been trained by our literal Judeo-Christian heritage to think of our myths as either literally true or not true at all."[1] Activity even intermittently on a mythic level, then—for example, what a poet produces—is not really given any validity by many of today's denizens of the world because the poet or artist basically is enacting symbolic play, the meaning of which is not literal. The fact that this cuts out or neutralizes a good deal of what the mind can do is not even considered, and a universal condition skirting boredom follows not far behind.

An amusing though prevalent attitude concerning Carlos Castaneda's Don Juan books precisely illuminates what I am talking about. Not too long ago, a friend of mine brought up the fact that a lot of people had begun to question whether the entire sequence of magical occurrences related by Castaneda had ever taken place at all. Certain stylistic and geographical factors seemed to allow for doubt. Were Don Juan and Don Genaro merely figments of Castaneda's imagination? So many people have read these books and been influenced by them that the possibility he was making it all up becomes dramatic. The inference, of course, is that if he made it up he was fooling us, and the books—as well as the entire spectrum of what was related in them—become worthless.

Leaving aside the possible ethical question involved—if he made it up and pretended he didn't, he was lying to his readers—the important point is the universal assumption that if something takes place in the outside world it is real, whereas if it is "dreamed up" then there is no validity involved, or, at most, it qualifies as entertainment. Maybe because I'm a poet myself, I find this attitude peculiar in the extreme. Since all knowledge is ultimately personal anyway, this narrow, reductive bias allows for only the crudest relationship to consciousness. The joke is that manipulation, like any belief system, functions as a myth, yet is assumed to be the only basis for what is real.

It's no surprise, therefore, that as contemporary civilization took its form over the last few centuries with the birth of the scientific and industrial revolutions, those people, such as poets, who fitfully operated from what can be called a mythic level of consciousness, found themselves ostracized from society. The Romantic movement in the nineteenth century may be viewed to an extent as a revolt against the increasingly meaningless position in which the artist was placed, and resolved itself as time went on into, for example, aggressive or virulently nonsensical stances taken by Surrealist and related artistic movements in the early part of this century.

I think, at this point, it is valuable to pull back and take a look at what imagination meant for earlier cultures, especially in terms of how this now-neglected faculty formed a central part of what various people actually experienced.

Originally, imagination in the form of shamanistic activity and mythical imagery was the factor that held all of life together—myths explained not only how the world came into being but also furnished the basic guidelines for orientation and identity within the world. In tribal life it was through visions that the content of myth was transmitted to the people. In a sense, however, their direct experience of something with a larger viewpoint than their own depended totally on the imagination, even if they weren't aware of it in such terms.

But visionary experience as transmitted to and shared by tribal cultures had an entirely different character than what takes place in the mind of some strung-out, drug-eating poet who operates by himself, because it was something shared and valued by all. This is an important point—not only the use it was put to, but the very nature of the imagination was radically other in tribal situations. It was socially shared experience rather than isolated artistic invention.

To quote from the *Edda*, the collection of ancient Icelandic sagas:

The unbreakable fetters which bound down the Great
Wolf Fenrir had been cunningly forged by Loki from
these: the footfall of a cat, the roots of a rock, the beard
of a woman, the breath of a fish, the spittle of a bird.[2]

What this creation myth says is that the order in life was
and still is secured by things which are intangible—in other
words, by elements rising out of the imagination. By "order"
there is no reason why we can't mean perception of reality
itself. The Great Wolf Fenrir is a figure of primeval chaos
or disorder, and world-origin myths almost always are
concerned with bringing order out of chaos (dark sea). But
the footfall of a cat, the roots of a rock, the beard of a
woman, etc., are fantastic things: things exactly the opposite
from what are encountered in an everyday sense. They're
things which don't exist, in other words, so that in essence
what we are talking about is mystery, and this myth states
that mystery is the basic cause for order in the universe. I
am rocked back by this.

In a real sense, then, imaginative activity itself—what
cannot be explained—is responsible for what *can* be explained. You can't have one without the other. The imagination as represented by these things (footfall of a cat, etc.)
presents elements of what's known in astronomy as an "anti-
world," the reverse or completion or other side of this life,
of value precisely because it cannot be explained.

Giorgio di Santillana and Hertha von Dechend, in writing
about traditional oracular activity and the language of
myth, say that, "The main merit of this language has turned
out to be its built-in ambiguity. Myth can be used as a vehicle for handing down solid knowledge independent from
the degree of insight of the people who do the actual telling
of stories, fables, etc."[3] Mythological lore was often transmitted by means of language, whose full meaning was known
only to higher initiates. Myth or esoteric doctrine "was
learned before being understood. Understanding remained
something apart. It might never come at all."[4]

Myth requires attention, not explanation. The great distance between tribal and modern levels of participation in consciousness is revealed by this fact. "In mystery rites there were things which 'could not be said' but only acted out. . . . Magic and mantic implications were present always in the business of the poet."[5] It is obvious, on the other hand, that myopic reduction of phenomena to only what is "provable" excludes allowing other levels of experience—the imaginative or invisible. As we notice in the *Edda*, imagination brings an order of participation to the world.

We can follow up this observation by looking at a book called *The Wizard of the Upper Amazon* by F. Bruce Lamb. This is the story (told later in life to the author) of Manuel Córdova-Rios, a Peruvian *curandero* or healer, who relates events that occurred around the turn of the century when he was about fifteen years old.

He traveled deep into the Amazon jungle on a rubber tapping expedition with two or three men, and one morning they woke to find themselves surrounded by a group of Indians who killed the others and took Manuel on a six-day forced march through the jungle to their village. He was held captive for seven years, and the book is a narration of his experiences. At first he thought he too would be killed, but soon he realized that he was being groomed very slowly by the old chief to take over leadership of the tribe. This was for a series of reasons, the most important being that the chief wanted guns to defend the tribe from other, hostile Indians. He needed the young Peruvian to teach his warriors to tap rubber, which Manuel then would transport alone to a trading post and exchange for arms and ammunition, since only a white man could buy guns. But the fascinating parts of the book are concerned with how the chief set about reprogramming the consciousness of this young, precocious white boy—a gradual but total initiation into Indian jungle life and the secret lore of the tribe by means of a series of sessions with a vision-producing extract of the jungle vine *ayahuasca* or *yagé,* called the vision vine. *Banisteriopsis caapi* is a powerful hallucinogen credited with the ability to release realms of experience where telepathy and clairvoyance are commonplace. Its effect is highly visual in nature.

But the key factor regarding the vision vine is that it always was taken in common with warriors of the tribe during special ceremonies conducted or orchestrated by the chief. They were group vision sessions, usually for the improvement of hunting, in which all participants saw the same detailed visions simultaneously. Therefore, Córdova's experiences with the vine consisted in shared consciousness with his captors.

The sessions were taken very seriously by the Indians involved. They were preceded by a week of fasting. The chief "prepared a series of combined herbal purges, baths and diet that had subtle effects on my feelings and bodily functions."[6] He would select certain persons he felt needed to improve as hunters and lead them to a special place in the forest. The soup made from the vine was produced in a meticulous manner, a sacred quality surrounding the entire procedure. After ingestion of the vine the chief would lead them all on a visual parade, as it were, in which everyone present *saw the same pictures* (more three-dimensional in nature than simply pictorial). By means of spoken chants and his own powers the chief caused a series of images to appear simultaneously before everyone; for example, a display of the animals of the forest that they hunted, down to the last detail. Birds they hunted, the male and female, their nests and mating patterns materialized—in vague outline at first, but soon with unimaginable detail. A normal sense of time disappeared also, as the vine took hold:

> With the chant of the boa, a giant constrictor appeared gliding slowly through the forest. Blue lights intensified an intricate design of scroll configurations that seemed to float along the boa's spine. Light flashed from his eyes and tongue. Bold patterns on the snake's skin glowed with intense and varied colors.

I was to learn later that the boa was greatly admired by these Indians for his ability to move silently through forest and capture other animals. The boa visions, brought on by a special chant, therefore came at the start of all seances dealing with the hunt. Other snakes followed the great boa—a giant bushmaster, a fer-de-lance, and many more.

Next came the birds, in particular members of the hawk family, thought to be the source of knowledge about the forest. With the special hawk chant there came first into the visions an enormous harpy eagle in flight, darting in and out through jungle vegetation. . . . Finally he alighted, spread his wings, displaying his creamy white breast and striped wings, then a jet-black back. Turning his head and raising his neck feathers into a magnificent crest, the eagle flashed baleful yellow eyes at us and snapped his beak.

Then a snake-eating hawk alighted and hopped around with wings spread downward, as when attacking a snake. He was followed by a parade of birds that served as sources of food. Each one repeated its various calls and displayed some characteristic of its habitat. . . .

Next came the animals, large and small, each with its own chant. The procession took all night and would be impossible for me to describe; much of it I no longer recall, since the knowledge did not originate from my consciousness or experience.[7]

These visions, from the tribal point of view, were absolutely practical in nature. They were meant to improve hunting ability, to re-integrate the hunter with the forest, and, as such, though dramatic and mysterious for all involved, they were a central activity as far as the tribe's everyday life was concerned. They were not "trips"; they were not seen as isolated, exotic experiencs.

One need only read, for example, William S. Burroughs' account in *The Yagé Letters* of taking the same vine, to realize the great gulf separating tribal and modern attitudes and uses of identical chemical substances.

Chief Xumu, with time's tradition still intact, directed the flow of visions into desired channels, an orientation obviously opposite to that within which Burroughs—taking the vine with a drunken, semi-civilized town *curandero*—was forced to operate. What Burroughs experienced, however revelatory, took place devoid of meaningful context. There was no way that what he saw could be integrated into the cultural reality preceding and following his trip. Contrast that fact with the following account, when Manuel is being groomed for eventual chieftainship:

> This was a period of intensive training for me. Once every eight days I would have a session of visions with the chief. These included examination of plants and their various uses, as well as further study of the animals. During the time between sessions I was taken often to the forest. On these excursions I found to my delight that the intensified awareness of surroundings originating in sessions with the chief stayed with me.
>
> After each series of four sessions I would have an equivalent period to absorb new experience and knowledge. A strict diet was still kept up, and then another series of vision sessions would begin. In actuality he was transmitting the accumulated tribal knowledge of, perhaps, centuries. At times during all this, which went on for months, I became nervous, high-strung and afraid of going insane. The chief noticed this and took pains to reassure me that as long as I followed the diets and instructions everything would come out well.[8]

As the training progressed, Manuel became aware of subtle changes in his modes of thought, including experiences of clairvoyance that allowed him to anticipate events and even divine the reactions and purposes of individuals in the tribe. Chief Xumu made him aware that this faculty was all-important to the governing of the tribe, and that his power to anticipate future events would improve with time.

It is interesting, also, to speculate about the nervous

mechanisms underlying the visionary process. As Andrew Weil writes in the introduction to Córdova's account, "The visual cortex of the brain seems implicated for several reasons. One is that it is the natural source of alpha waves, those frequencies that seem to correlate with meditative states and certain kinds of psychic phenomena."[9] The visual cortex seems to produce this rhythm only when it is not occupied with interpretation of signals coming from the eyes:

> What we see when our visual cortex is interpreting signals from somewhere other than the retina might have more to tell us about the nature of reality. This idea might be upsetting to those who refuse to believe in realities other than the one of consensus we use for convenience. The Indians described in this book consider the visionary world as real as the ordinary one; they are able to go there together. . . . What the partaker of *ayahuasca* sees in the visions is dependent not on the drug but on other factors: the mood and setting of the group, the physical and mental states of the participants, and above all the chanting of the leader of the ritual. Many persons who take hallucinogens have experienced the special relationship between sound and visions, but Chief Xumu's use of chants to bring on an orderly, logically developing sequence of visions is a highly evolved power.[10]

One developmental psychologist has concluded that perception and imagination arise from a common faculty in the nervous system and were originally identical.[11]

This visionary experience, then, was not exotic. Gringo individuals going down to South America, getting ripped out of their skulls and ending up staring at the sky certainly have unique adventures. But they are divorced from a social context, whereas in this tribe experiences contained shared definitions among a group of people who together comprised the reality of their village. Imagination was integrated within everyday tribal life, rather than being a spectral instance of something.

Whereas the modern way of dealing with mythic imagination—whether resulting from visions, dreams, or, for that matter, issuing from states described as mentally ill—seems to keep its symbols private, autistic and undeveloped, tribal attitudes encourage public, symbolic enactment. In many tribal cultures, "The enactment of dreams is all-important as a therapeutic technique. Dreams are believed to ask for a making-real, either through a literal enactment of what the dream wants to do, or by means of symbolic masked ritual."[12] The key difference, again, is one of context. The entire range of mythic symbols functions as a kind of vocabulary in the most obvious sense—it allows something to be said.

Shamanistic tradition of violent out-of-body experience, for example, has to be viewed within the context of our culture as psychotic behavior, whereas the shaman himself is not at all psychotic. He is a functional member of his particular social order, and his tribe participates, through ritual, in the shaman's trance adventure. As Stephen Larsen writes, "We have no symbolic vocabulary, no mythological tradition to make our own experiences comprehensible to us. We have, in fact, no senior shamans to help ensure that our dismemberment be followed by a rebirth."[13]

In contemporary societies, abstract categorical thinking is given full attention or validity, while mythic or imaginative thinking is ignored, neglected, considered superficial. As we have seen, the way in which imaginative activity was approached by tribal cultures points up this difference. To quote from Joseph Campbell:

> In the primitive world gods and demons are not conceived as hard and fast, positive realities. The phenomenon of the primitive mask is a case in point. The mask is revered as an apparition of the mythical being it represents, yet everyone knows that a man made the mask and that a man is wearing it. . . .

In other words there has been a shift of view from the logic of the normal secular sphere, where things are understood to be distinct from each other, to a theatrical or play sphere, where they are accepted for what they are experienced as being, and the logic is that of "make-believe"—"as if."

The world is hung with banners. The logic of cold, hard fact must not be allowed to intrude and spoil the spell. The gentile, the "spoilsport," the positivist who cannot or will not play, must be kept aloof. Hence the guardian figures that stand at the entrances to holy places: lions, bulls or fearsome warriors with uplifted weapons. They are there to keep out the spoilsports, the advocates of Aristotelian logic, for whom A can never be B; for whom the actor is never lost in his part; for whom the mask, the image, the consecrated tree or animal is only a reference. For the whole purpose of entering a sanctuary or participating in a festival is to be . . . set apart from one's logic of self-possession and overpowered by the force of a logic of indissociation, where A is B, and C is also B.[14]

I'd like to resume this discussion by returning to the modern world, more or less, in the form of reading a prose poem called "Childhood" from the *Illuminations* by Arthur Rimbaud. Please note—in addition to rich imagery and magical participation by the poet in his created world—the uncanny resemblance of Part III to the section quoted earlier from the *Edda*:

I

That idol, black eyes and yellow mop, without parents or court, nobler than Mexican and Flemish fables; his domain, insolent azure and verdure, runs over beaches called by the shipless waves, names ferociously Greek, Slav, Celt.

At the border of the forest—dream flowers tinkle,

flash and flare—the girl with orange lips, knees crossed in the clear flood that gushes from the fields, nakedness shaded, traversed, dressed by rainbow, flora, sea.

Ladies who stroll on terraces adjacent to the sea; baby girls and giantesses, superb blacks in the verdigris moss, jewels upright on the rich ground of groves and little thawed gardens—young mothers and big sisters with eyes full of pilgrimages, sultanas, princesses tyrannical of costume and carriage, little foreign misses and young ladies gently unhappy.

What boredom, the hour of the "dear body" and "dear heart."

II

It is she, the little girl dead behind the rose-bushes.—The young mamma, deceased, comes down the stoop.—The cousin's carriage creaks on the sand.—The little brother (he is in India!) there, before the western sky in the meadow of pinks. The old men who have been buried upright in the rampart overgrown with gillyflowers.

Swarms of golden leaves surround the general's house. They are in the south.—You follow the red road to reach the empty inn. The château is for sale; the shutters are coming off. The priest must have taken away the key of the church. Around the park the keepers' cottages are uninhabited. The enclosures are so high that nothing can be seen but the rustling tree tops. Besides, there is nothing to be seen within.

The meadows go up to the hamlets without anvils or cocks. The sluice gate is open. O the Calvaries and the windmills of the desert, the islands and the haystacks!

Magic flowers droned. The slopes cradled him. Beasts of a fabulous elegance moved about. The clouds gathered over the high sea, formed of an eternity of hot tears.

III

In the woods there is a bird; his song stops you and makes you blush.

There is a clock that never strikes.

There is a hollow with a nest of white beasts.

There is a cathedral that goes down and a lake that goes up.

There is a little carriage abandoned in the copse or that goes running down the road beribboned.

There is a troupe of little actors in costume, glimpsed on the road through the border of the woods.

And then, when you are hungry and thirsty, there is someone who drives you away.

IV

I am the saint at prayer on the terrace like the peaceful beasts that graze down to the sea of Palestine.

I am the scholar of the dark armchair. Branches and rain hurl themselves at the windows of my library.

I am the pedestrian of the highroad by way of the dwarf woods; the roar of the sluices drowns my steps. I can see for a long time the melancholy wash of the setting sun.

I might well be the child abandoned on the jetty on its way to the high seas, the little farm boy following the lane, its forehead touching the sky.

The paths are rough. The hillocks are covered with broom. The air is motionless. How far away are the birds and the springs! It can only be the end of the world ahead.

V

Let them rent me this whitewashed tomb, at last, with cement lines in relief—far down under the ground.

I lean my elbows on the table, the lamp shines brightly on these newspapers I am fool enough to read again, these stupid books.

At an enormous distance above my subterranean parlor, houses take root, fogs gather. The mud is red or black. Monstrous city, night without end!

Less high are the sewers. At the sides, nothing but the thickness of the globe. Chasms of azure, wells of fire perhaps. Perhaps it is on these levels that moons and comets meet, fables and seas.

In hours of bitterness, I imagine balls of sapphire, of metal. I am master of silence. Why should the semblance of an opening pale under one corner of the vault?[15]

Rimbaud's work was characterized by a highly compressed, highly volatile use of imagination, I'm sure you'll agree, and yet the figure of Rimbaud as poet—the image this word stood for in the society in which he lived—is just as important to explore as is the work itself. The poet inhabits a rich, exciting world divorced, however, from any positive relationship to the rest of society ("What boredom," "formed of an eternity of hot tears," "And then there is someone who drives you away") and culminating in a total retreat ("It can only be the end of the world ahead." "Let them rent me this whitewashed tomb") . The special state of mind pursued is identified with childhood; and the altered states of time, the mingling of past and present, the occasional distortions of syntactical structure approach mythic or visionary levels of consciousness. But childhood is seen as a vanishing commodity, a state of grace threatened by the passage of time.

Although Rimbaud's writing and rebellious stance as an artist came as a reaction to the Romantic movement that grew throughout the nineteenth century, he in some way still represented, or carried several steps further, a modern image of the poet that was born with that movement in France and elsewhere.

The Romantic movement in itself is very interesting. Why did it spring up at the beginning of the nineteenth century? Why do we suddenly have generations of artists whose stance toward their creativity and surroundings involved being feverish, instead of controlled, with their imagination? As the parameters of the industrial revolution became defined, poets seemed to find themselves victimized by the very fact that they possessed a working imagination. Then, of course, they began to develop a myth about that victimization, victimization becoming a prime Romantic response, which they sort of folded into more and more. (Baudelaire's *Paris Spleen,* published at mid-century, being the literary turning-point: no one had expressed dissatisfaction and even revulsion with the modern world in quite the same terms before.) Early on one reached the level of, for example, the life of Gerard de Nerval, a delicate and beautiful poet whose erratic, unbalanced behavior—leading a lobster on a blue silk leash through the Luxembourg Gardens—resulted in his eventually hanging himself in a gutter, broken and broke. The artist as tragic hero.

But, as Walter Benjamin writes in his surprising study of Baudelaire and his era, Baudelaire (as well as Balzac) encountered the life and atmosphere of modern urban populations to such a penetrating degree that he outgrew attitudes of Romanticism and in the process became the first poet to really meet the modern age head-on, to see poets as a race whose days are numbered:

The hero is the true subject of modernism. In other words, it takes a heroic constitution to live modernism. With his belief, Baudelaire is in opposition to Romanticism. He transfigures passions and resolution; the Romantics transfigured renunciation and surrender.

What the man working for wages achieves in his daily work is no less than what in ancient times helped a gladiator win applause and fame. This image is one of the best insights that Baudelaire had; it derives from his reflection about his own situation. A passage from the "Salon de 1859" indicates how he wanted to have it viewed: "When I hear how a Raphael or a Veronese are glorified with the veiled intention of depreciating what

came after them . . . I ask myself whether an
achievement which must be rated *at least* equal to
theirs . . . is not infinitely *more meritorious,* because
it triumphed in a hostile environment and place.[16]

The Romantic image was really a syndrome of how poetic
imagination is taken in a society, how it is used. If it is re-
jected, if it falls outside the pragmatic reality which alone is
considered to have substance, this psychological reaction is
inevitable. In a mercantile situation where something must
enter the marketplace before it is seen and valued, poetic or
artistic imagination survives only when translated into entertainment: or, as in the case of paintings, into things which
can be bought and sold as objects, for reasons of social
status, and so forth.

Tracking the evolution of the artistic image in French society, to take a clear example, one sees how this process
could culminate in the early twentieth century in the Dada
and Surrealist movements, in poets such as Tristan Tzara
who reached the point of saying the entire straight world is
a hallucination and we're going to make you see that by
turning everything upside-down and writing works that are
aggressively nonsensical, and by telling you that you are
all—the lives you lead, the manners and prejudices you live
by—completely full of shit; in fact, by screaming it from the
rooftops. Or consider the life of Raymond Roussel, literary
inventor of parallel worlds and master of purely abstract
methodologies, whose aesthetic creed became: "The work
must contain nothing real, no observation on the world, the
mind, nothing but completely imaginary combinations."

But Rimbaud is especially interesting for another reason.
In modern societies imagination seems to be tied in some
special way with adolescence. I remember being told, when
I started writing poetry, that everyone writes some poetry
when they're eighteen years old—if I was still writing when I
was thirty, that's when I could be considered "a real case."
You're in the ballpark of visionary reality, to a greater or
lesser degree, until you reach adulthood, whereupon this

fades out as you become a responsible member of society. You go to work in a hardware store, you become a lawyer or housewife, and the rest drops away.

Rimbaud's life was an extreme version of this pattern. He wrote, he left home, his private life was very turbulent, and before his twenty-second birthday he stopped writing. Actively renouncing as outmoded any attempt to continue producing literature, Rimbaud spent the rest of his life—to be sure, in his own unpredictable fashion—meeting the world as engineer, white trader and gun runner in some of the harshest, most inhospitable places on earth: at Aden on the Red Sea and in the Ogaden wastelands of what is now Ethiopia. At age thirty-seven he contracted what was diagnosed as carcinoma, but might have been syphilis, returned to France where a leg was amputated, and died shortly thereafter.

The revelatory fact is that beginning the year before his death he had written home to his mother requesting scientific books, and on his deathbed bitterly repeated his desire to have a son and teach him technology and the practical sciences. This represents, obviously, a complete turn-around from his early life as a poet, and is another way of saying that all he wanted was to find a place in the real world, and that he saw poetry and, correspondingly, imaginative activity, in general, as a dead end in those terms.

Childhood has been seen for some time as a relatively blessed or magical period which disappears with the development of one's adult identity. In a short story by Colette called "The Priest on the Wall," the author observes her daughter's behavior and recalls an incident from her own childhood. The eight-year-old Colette "became" a priest when she happened to hear a word she didn't know. Instead of asking an adult for its definition, she went off to the top of the garden wall where she played alone and allowed her imagination free reign:

> The word "presbytery" had chanced that year to drop into my sensitive ears and had wrought havoc.

"It's undoubtedly the most cheerful presbytery that I
know of. . . ." someone had said in my hearing.

Far from asking one of my relations: "What is a
presbytery?" I had absorbed the mysterious word with
its harsh and spiky beginning and the brisk trot of its final syllables. Enriched by a secret and a doubt, I slept
on the *word* and bore it off to my wall. "Presbytery!" I
would shout it over the roof of the hen house and
Miton's garden, toward the perpetually misty horizon of
Moutiers. From the summit of my wall, the word rang
out as a malediction: "Begone! You are all presby-
teries!" I shouted to invisible outlaws.

Later on, the word lost some of its venom and I began to suspect that "presbytery" might very possibly be
the scientific term for a certain little yellow-and-black-
striped snail. A chance remark was to be my undoing,
in one of those moments when a child, however solemn
or fanciful she might be, fleetingly resembles the picture made of her by grown-up people.

"Mother! Look what a lovely little presbytery I've
found!"

"A lovely little—what?"

"A lovely little presby—"

I broke off, but too late. I had to learn—"I sometimes
wonder if this child is all there"—that of which I was so
anxious to remain in ignorance, and to "call things by
their proper names . . ."[17]

The light charm of this story does not disguise the fact
that there exists a definite division between childhood and
adulthood in terms of relation to the outside, bringing up
the problem of the disappearance of imagination with the
fade-in to name, family and job.

It seems to me that a serious struggle taking place in
modern society today is due to this split between
"personality" (nine-to-five job, public occupation, public
face, name in the phone book) and any really gratifying, energetic integration with mythic or imaginative levels of

being. As Walter Benjamin comments, "The resistance which modernism offers to the natural productive élan of a person is out of proportion to his strength."[18]

The imagination today might not denote the opposite of usefulness, but it uses objects comprising the reality of this world in a different way from how it is structured in every other sense. In the simplest terms, everyday reality means that when you're driving down Main Street and see a stop light, you respond, and when it turns green, you go. But once imagination is involved, you could be dealing with that street and that stop light in ways that have little to do with the practical options you've been taught or restricted to since infancy, even while continuing to drive down the same old street!

As the supposed Don Juan explains to the supposed Carlos Castaneda in *Tales of Power,* what one sees throughout life is never the world itself but a description of the world ·issuing exclusively from reason, from only one level of response. It is up to us whether we are willing to view participation in imagination not simply as art but as life, open to variation and growth; whether each of us is willing to ask ourselves: do I accept the pure products of my mind as real?

> Today I have to pound the nail that Genaro put in, the fact that we are luminous beings. We are perceivers. We are an awareness; we are not objects; we have no solidity. We are boundless. The world of objects and solidity is a way of making our passage on earth convenient. It is only a description that was created to help us. We, or rather our *reason,* forget that the description is only a description and thus we entrap the totality of ourselves in a vicious circle from which we rarely emerge in our lifetime.[19]

Notes

1. Stephen Larsen, *The Shaman's Doorway* (New York: Harper & Row, 1976) , p. 121.
2. G. de Santillana and H. von Dechend, *Hamlet's Mill* (Boston: Gambit Press, 1969) , p. 9.
3. Ibid., p. 312.
4. Ibid., p. 118.
5. Ibid., p. 119.
6. From *Wizard of the Upper Amazon* by F. Bruce Lamb and Manuel Cordoba. Copyright ©1971, 1974 by F. Bruce Lamb. Reprinted by permission of Houghton Mifflin Company, for distribution in the United States, Canada, and the Philippines. Permission granted by Bertha Klausner International Literary Agency, Inc., for distribution throughout the English-speaking world.
7. Ibid., pp. 37-39.
8. Ibid., pp. 96-97.
9. Ibid., p. vii.
10. Ibid., p. ix.
11. Larsen, op. cit., p. 49.
12. Ibid, p. 89.
13. Ibid., p. 81.
14 Joseph Campbell, "The Historical Development of Mythology," *Myth and Mythmaking*, ed., Henry Murray (Boston: Beacon Press, 1968) , pp. 33, 40.
15. Arthur Rimbaud, *Illuminations*, trans. by Louise Varèse. Copyright © 1946, 1957 by New Directions Publishing Corporation. Reprinted by permission of New Directions Publishing Corporation.
16. Walter Benjamin, *Charles Baudelaire: A Lyric Poet in the Era of High Capitalism* (London: NLB, 1973) , pp. 74-75.
17. Colette, *Gigi and Selected Writings* (New York: New American Library, Signet, 1963) , p. 53.
18. Benjamin, op. cit., p. 75.
19. Carlos Castaneda, *Tales of Power* (New York: Pocket Books, 1976) , p. 97.

Photo by Blair Hansen

Philip Whalen

SUDDEN HISTORIES, NATURAL JUMPS

JULY 23, 1976

WHAT I REMEMBERED the other day was, somebody said, "Why do I have to read all these books in order to understand anything or write anything?" The answer is in a book by the late Ben Jonson, who was a contemporary of Shakespeare. The book is called *Explorata*, or *Discoveries*. (*Timber* is the popular name.) This edition of Jonson, a very handy one, is a Penguin edition. It has modernized spelling. There's an American edition by W. W. Norton that reproduces the old spelling; you can pick up on what it was Jonson was seeing when he was writing, and what people were looking at when they were reading him, if you look at the old spelling edition. There's yet a third edition from Oxford Press which contains one more item, namely, the *Leges Conviviales*, the laws for the people who like to have fun together, that Jonson wrote in Latin. It's a long poem about how poets should get along together when they're sitting up there in the tavern, where they used to eat and drink. But this particular edition is interesting because it has all the poems in it, it has the *Timber* and the translation from Horace and what not.

But in any case a propos of what you have to know, "for a man to write well," he says, "there are required three necessities: to read the best authors, observe the best speakers, and much exercise of his own style. In styles to consider what ought to be written, and after what manner, he must first think and excogitate his matter, then choose his words and examine the weight of either. Then take care in placing and ranking both matter and words, that the composition be comely, and to do this with diligence and often. . . ." And later Jonson says, "The reason why a poet is said, that he ought to have all knowledges, is that he should not be ignorant of the most, especially of those he will handle. And indeed, when the attaining of them is possible, it were a sluggish and base thing to despair. For frequent imitation of anything becomes a habit quickly. If a man should prosecute as much as could be said of everything, his work would find no end."

Anyway, Jonson was always reading. At one point his house caught fire and burned his library. He was in a very bad state and wrote the "Execration upon Vulcan." King James very kindly gave him a whole lot of money to replace a few of the books, at that time they were extremely expensive and very hard to get. So much for the connection between reading and writing.

I was asking you to think about the first poems and about early poetry as a social phenomenon, when people were less organized then they are now, or differently organized, in what we think of as a tribal society. When we look fondly for the past, what do we find, we don't find it at all. We don't find the past, we don't find The Primitive. We're older than we imagine, the universe is older. For a long time it was popular to suppose that the universe was created by the hand of God in October of the year 4004 B. C., and it was a nice day, we're told. This information comes to us from an Irish Archbishop, so it must be true. His name was Usher. His descendants of that name now make a very good whiskey. For a long time it was imagined that the earth was not terribly old and that people were, what, seven days younger than the earth and had been educated by angels and then had fallen, and that the world was destroyed by flood and fire and reconstituted afterwards, and here we all sit, wonderfully restored, wonderfully saved by the appearance of Jesus, who showed everybody the right way to live and to be. Here we are.

On the other hand, there are all those other people out there. All those funny pagans and "lesser breeds without the Law" as Mr. Kipling said. They don't worship properly, they aren't Christians, they're different. We can't understand them when they talk, just like several millennia ago the Greeks said, "All those guys over there are barbarians, they go ba ba ba ba ba ba, all the time, they can't talk plain, they don't talk Greek."

So it is with us. We say, "Well, those horrible people over there are not Christians, and I can't understand them. They're eating each other. They don't wear clothes. We better go civilize them. We'd better go and save them and get them all dipped properly, and made into good Christians. Everything will be a lot better when they can stop being primitive creatures, they can stop being savages, they can build automobiles and listen to TV, and do all the things that nice people do. Everybody should be like us, and anybody who isn't like us is a savage, quasi-animal, "Wild Man of the Woods," something like that. This attitude prevailed in Western society for a good many years, and still does to a certain extent.

In the late eighteenth century, people started looking around a little differently, and Jean-Jacques Rousseau and some other people came out and said, "Huh! Maybe we're not so sharp. Maybe we aren't doing it so good. Maybe we've all been depraved and wrecked and had our minds all twisted by the social arrangements which now prevail, which ought to be taken apart and thrown out, because, actually, people left to themselves are noble savages. Like the Indians in the Americas and the South Sea Islanders who live the simple elegant life. They go around picking their food off trees, and they're sweet to each other, and they dress in leaves if they dress at all, and they're natural—absolutely natural—just like the natural foods store, where you have to pay seventy-five cents for a lemon. Natural."

This was the big pitch: human beings are groovy from the start, then you expose them to laws and schools and social systems and their heads get all funny. They become sad people, who presently turn to wickedness and vice and crime for amusement, instead of thinking of eating oranges and bananas off the tree. Next, they're stealing and murdering and carrying on in all sorts of unattractive ways.

Later on, of course, we got into the feeling that maybe we were mistaken about the "savage" business. We did some investigating and found out that some of the "savages" had really rather complicated and marvelous ways of dealing with their own environment and with each other, and they were actually getting along quite wonderfully until the Christians came along and made them wear muumuus, so that they all got tuberculosis and died.

In the Marianna Islands, they stopped breeding because they said, "We've been wrecked by these horrible white men, and we're not going to buy it, and we're going to stop," and did. The anthropologists gradually got into the idea about how maybe *we* were ethnocentric, we who were looking at these so-called savages were completely bent by our own training into imagining *we* were right, and everybody else was wrong. We thought that our way of doing things was the center of the world and how everybody else was supposed to be. We started springing our heads out in various directions and seeing maybe we were not perfect. Something like that. Maybe our system wasn't the very best. Instead of using the terms "savage" or "pagan" or "heathen" or whatnot, the terms "preliterate" or "nonliterate" peoples came into vogue. And I suppose that schools of anthropology, that grew up around people like Franz Boas and Ruth Benedict et al., are responsible for this shift. Mr. Benjamin Whorf had the idea that if people were illiterate it wasn't so important. Even though they didn't have a written literature, they might have a very long oral one, all sorts of epics and myths and stories and songs, which were very carefully preserved and passed from generation to generation. Much of it poetry—material in rhyming verse—was easier to memorize.

For memorizing things, like who one's great-grandfather was, a rhythmical chain of genealogies was a common kind of poem that people learned in the South Seas. For example, the royal lineage would be memorized—all those names. A story about why goats breed in the wintertime would be a metrical composition passed on from one goatherder to another, from time immemorial. They never got around to writing it down, even though they had developed a writing system. In addition to that kind of information, it turned out that the so-called savages had very complicated kinds of social orders—how you treat your mother-in-law, what sort of initiation rites you go through when you turned adolescent, what sort of funeral rites are celebrated when somebody dies—all unwritten. People made it up as they went along.

It's very hard to figure out how old this poetry was before any of it was being written down. The oldest records that we have are from the Mesopotamian area, where they wrote in cuneiform on clay tablets that were baked up and saved. But those are belated records of much earlier material, probably, just as the Iliad and the Odyssey were written down many centuries after they started being sung. The epics were composed several centuries after the alleged actions were taking place. Homer wasn't there watching what was happening, but was telling stories that were around, that everybody knew, composing these into poems. All of this is much later, the writing of them, setting them into the regular twenty-four-book system, is a late manifestation. Goodness knows what the Bible must have been like before it got regularized and revamped and fixed up, because there are so many reflections in it of the earlier religion that prevailed in that area, that it must have been quite different from what we have. Sir James G. Frazer wrote a book all about that called, *Folklore in the Old Testament*, and a lot more work has been done since his time, by Theodore Gaster and Samuel Noah Kramer.

People sang because they were happy or unhappy, or

quite often because there was some guy there, shaman-witch-doctor-priest-poet, who said, "All right, we're all gonna sing now because George is dead," and they said, "What do we sing, what do we sing?" and the poet would say, "Well, then now, ah! The Ancestors tell me that George's spirit is right over there and he likes to sing about the crab apple blossoms in the springtime." Everybody says, "Oh yeah?" And the poet looks cross-eyed and heavenwards and asks, "Isn't that right, George? OK. 'Crab apple Blossoms in the Springtime' followed shortly thereafter by the 'Salmon Catching Song,' if you please." And everybody looks around and says, "What's all this about?" And the medicine man, who is laying the story on them, says, "All right, everybody listen now: 'O the crab apple blossoms in the valley, ha ha'—All right, everybody line up now, in honor of George," and of course the corpse is all laid out on the ground and painted with ochre, and flowers around his neck, and maybe some beads and pots beside him, and everybody starts marching around, "O the crab apple . . ." You've got a song and dance. Presumably, they care enough about George to do this—the late George is an object of some concern to them. It'll make them feel better, especially George's family and cousins who are feeling kind of sad. It gives them something to do, to march around and sing. The reason that you hop around on one foot is that it goes in with the crab apple somehow, tramping out the crab apple juice perhaps, I don't know. Anyway, some sort of rhythmical physical activity goes along with the beat of the song. The next day, these benighted savages are out there wondering what they're going to do next, when all of a sudden the Egyptians come along, and the Egyptians says, "All right you guys, come on over here. We're going to build this pyramid." And our tribe says, "Well, what's a pyramid?" And the Egyptians say, "Well, you come on with us, and you'll find out." So presently, here is the same tribe (now without George) all lined up pulling this rock. They're working, and pulling on something, and singing in order to forget the fact that the sun is hot, and they haven't had very much to eat, and it's a boring job, and they're thinking about crab apples in the distance, and they're far away from that place now. The Egyptians are only giving them a little bit of weak beer and onions to eat, no crab apples, and it's sad. And so by the waters of whatever, they're sitting and weeping, having to pull rocks around. You get another thing going, of words and music and action, all happening together.

Sources

FRAZER, SIR JAMES, *Folklore in the Old Testament* (New York: Hart Pub. Co., 1965).

JONSON, BEN, "Timber: or Discoveries," *The Complete Poems* (Great Britain: Printed by Hazell Watson and Vinly Ltd., Aylesbury, Bucks: A Division of Penguin Books, Ltd.).

Jerome Rothenberg

CHANGING THE PRESENT, CHANGING THE PAST: A NEW POETICS

AUGUST 10, 1976

I ONCE SAID, I think it was in *Shaking the Pumpkin,* something about teaching poetry classes with a rattle and a drum, a rattle *or* a drum. I said it, you know prematurely, 'cause I wasn't using a rattle then. But shortly thereafter, in order to get across in an immediate way things that I'd seen happening in Seneca poetry, I began to sing some of the songs in English translation, and I've come in the process of singing them to learn much more about them and to find that they have a way of calming me, exhausting and calming me, a simultaneous process. So, before getting into that part of the session which is largely talk and reading, I'll take off from the notion that poetry, although converted to books, precedes writing, precedes a literate tradition, that poetry goes back to our earliest beginnings as human beings and continues in some kind of unbroken line up to the present, in which writing is, I would take it, both a complication and another possibility. . . . And starting from that notion, I'll sing a few songs, and maybe others would want to join in on it. I usually do it by myself, but there's absolutely no reason for that. The original songs, in the place where these songs come from, would be sung by a single ceremonial leader in a ceremony called "shaking the pumpkin," the work of a medicine society sometimes called, I suppose by nineteenth-century anthropologists who were first charting that thing, the "Society of the Mystic Animals," a lovely name. But in Seneca, the word used is *I'dos,* which is not translatable as anything else but the name of that society, the medicine society in that ceremony. So, mystic animals, the animals of the ceremony, are called into the sacred precinct at the beginning. And the first song, if translated, goes something like this: [*He shakes a rattle and sings, ends up breathless after a final, extended exhalation.*]

Sometimes I don't know if that leaves me in a position to talk or not. I keep thinking that it does. The situation, of course, in many ways seems to be totally transformed here from the way in which that song goes, how those poems would be delivered back there. Back there is the northeast, in what's still a woodland area along the southern tier in New York, the New York-Pennsylvania border, at the Allegheny-Seneca reservation, the place that the Senecas in fact began to settle fairly late along, when they themselves were sending young men out as pioneer groups. The movement of the Europeans was also, of course, causing other kinds of early movements, and this area along the Allegheny River was a Seneca pioneer settlement, a frontier settlement, so to speak. It wasn't their residence; they might have gone in there at first for hunting reasons, but the earlier settlement was further east, in the Geneseo area, and only later on they moved. They settled at Allegheny and over into Pennsylvania under the influence of the great chief, Corn Planter. And that's become *the* place, now set aside as "reservation," a thin narrow strip along the Allegheny River, a mile wide on each side, extending, I think, for forty-one or forty-two miles. There are still animals in the vicinity, and some of the people still trace their lineage, heritage, from animal ancestors through an ongoing clan system. But maybe more about that later.

When I first started writing, specifically writing poetry, I wouldn't have imagined myself in the situation of shaking a rattle and singing songs; I mean, one knew from early along a connection between poetry and song, but I think the going idea was that poetry becomes poetry when it separates itself from song . . . that it isn't poetry as long as it's part of a more complicated and unified system, but it becomes poetry as the voice moves away from the actual singing.

Yet poets even at that time were talking about their "music." David Antin, who's been a close friend for twenty years, even then found that terminology incomprehensible and still finds it, you know—*what kind of music are you talking about*, once that separation has been made? So Antin, in one of the interesting reconsiderations of poetry and where it all comes from, says, no, *not* from song, rather from discourse, from speech. You know, take that as another possibility. So I'm going to talk about some of the work that I've done, which is not completely my own work; I mean, it's the work of these various anthologies[1] [*he shows a number of books*] that begin to make a big pile, of whatever, and in a little while an even bigger pile. I'm assuming that some of you know one of these or two of these. . . . But I'll try a kind of run-through of what the intention was there, and how I think it ties in, very much ties in to the work of other contemporaries. So in that sense, it's not a personal work at all, although in other ways, you know, very personal, and increasingly personal. But when I say that Antin raises the possibility that poetry derives not from song, as some of us came later to believe, but from discourse, I put that in the context of a contemporary poetry that's been involved in raising possibilities about itself. Raising possibilities about poetry itself, and therefore laying itself open to the greater possibility of transformation and self-transformation, both for poetry, that great conglomerate body, and presumably for the individuals involved in the process, both as speakers, sounders, and as listeners, though it seems to me that what's been taking place is a convergence of the poet and the audience for poetry.

Philip Whalen quoted Walt Whitman on that slogan which used to be, maybe still is on the back cover of *Poetry* magazine: "In order to have great poets, great poetry, you

have to have great audiences." Now, though, there is a
possibility that ultimately what you move towards is . . .
why are there so many poets? Well, it must be that poetry is
developing into a condition in which there will be no
separation between poets and audience, so maybe that's not
a terrible thing when you say that someone's audience is
limited to poets. Well, I go around and give poetry readings,
and the audience is full of young poets or of people who do
poetry, make their own poetry, and where are the other
people? Well, maybe that's not a cause for alarm. I mean,
surely we can't all have decided to become poets because the
profession is so terrific and pays so well. . . . Just look
at the directory that *Poets and Writers* puts out: it's just a
small sampling of people seriously doing poetry in America,
I've never counted it out, but you know, there's a huge
gathering of names there. More individuals truly than the
market can bear, if it's a question of market in any sense.
Something else must be going on, and maybe that coming
together of, that literal identity of poet and audience may
ultimately, if it continues to proliferate, fulfill Blake's
prophecy. You know, he says—in a paraphrase from one of
the first five books of the Old Testament, a paraphrase that
seems to be implicit in William Blake's use of it—"Would
that all the children of the Lord, would that all God's
children were poets," or the original itself, "Would that all
God's children were prophets."

And right there is another of the interesting possibilities
that's raised, you know, by Blake primarily and then again
and again up to the present, a second convergence, a
convergence and identification of poetry and prophecy. So
Blake, looking back, recognizes the prophets not only as
prophets, which is a historical perspective, a fact in itself,
but as men of open and expensive senses that he can identify with the concept of the "poet" that he's developing.
Blake himself, in the sense of the word "prophetic" meaning—being able to look into the future—which is perhaps
a very minor notion of what prophecy is about but I think
we tend to think of it in those terms—Blake is being

prophetic in that sense towards one of the possibilities being explored today and throughout this century, throughout the last century as well, something hidden beneath the facade of poetry as a literary enterprise, which has even been dominant in cultures that can be literary, that can deal with letters and with writing. So I'll again and again use the term possibility, possibilities, opening possibilities and opening, you know, rather than closing . . . like closing the possibilities, bringing it down to a single answer . . . because more and more I feel that the reason for my own involvement with poetics, *poesis*, as a process, is that, of all the processes that I know for that kind of exploration of mind, or whatever, that people talk about, the poetic engagement, the poetic process, seems most to allow, when it's really working, most to allow room for contradiction and for conflict. The poetic liberty, the poetic *license*, you know, which was hammered into our heads even as kids, in a kind of derogatory way . . . *well so-&-so says that, that's a lie, that's poetic license.*

So in a sense the poet has had this license, has had it even in ages that were hostile to poetry, this privilege to create what the preservers of the conventional reality would take as a lie. The poet can make "lies," and for this Plato banished, would have banished the poets from the Republic, because at least at that point he chose to be obtuse to what was going on, though elsewhere, or maybe in the same context, he says, you know, but I too was once in love with poetry, I was once a poet myself. A little bit like Laura Riding in that sense, or Laura Riding a little bit like Plato in that sense, when she says that she's renouncing poetry, she's giving it up because the poet is ultimately a teller of lies; and she says he's a teller of lies because he does what poets so often do, pursues the truth by other means . . . means other than "logical." You know, those means that everyone associates with poetry, like, let's say, a pursuing of the truth by soundings. In other words, let sound lead you, make your way through music and all that. When sound leads you, you know, maybe you get to the same place, maybe you get to

another place; but if you're following that development
through Plato, Aristotle and the makers of European logic
and rationalism, it's a false pursuit. Yet for most poets I
know, if you ask what determines the next word, the moves
they make in the poem—well, in some sense the sound determines the next word. And what is it for the sound to determine, and so on? Is it *sound* for the sound to determine the
next word? Okay, those are, those are possibilities. But
remember, Plato and Laura Riding say, poetry—no, not
poetry . . . yeah, poetry . . . poetry a lying word
. . . poet a lying word! [*There is an interruption while a
tape recorder is being adjusted.*]

I'm haunted by technology. Technology at a certain
point became one of the other possibilities, but it's very dangerous. We were having a poetics conference at the University of Wisconsin in Milwaukee where I was teaching
temporarily, and I got into this rap about technology and I
said there's a danger in all of this, and I told the story of
being somewhere and giving a poetry reading at night and
the lights went out. There was a power failure, you know,
and when that power goes, if you gotta pick this book up
and read those words, you can only do it in daylight, there
are no night-time ceremonies at that point. You have to be
able to see it; if you're doing it at night you have to depend
on this system, and this system . . . I don't know how it
works, you know, but it's hooked into that wall, and it's controlled wherever the power comes from, but it's very far
away. So I was giving a poetry reading and the lights did go
out, you know, so what do I do? So I grabbed my trusty
rattle (I couldn't have done that some time ago when everything was in a book), and I began doing what I could do
without that outside power source. So I told this story in
Milwaukee, and a little bit later, I guess that same morning,
Nathaniel Tarn got up to deliver a written talk, and the
power went out. It was a big room with no windows, it was
dark, no microphones, you know, it was too large for him to
continue talking, so I said there must be something in it, the
way the same event repeats itself. It must be a warning. So I

think we should have some non-technological fail-safe, some-thing for emergency purposes, as my wife, remembering the death march in Bataan and people being carried off to concentration camps and so forth during the Second World War, my wife wants to be able to walk great distances, not for the the love of walking, just as a precautionary measure, if it ever comes to that.

Okay. In *America a Prophecy*, we're occasionally also into other, older modes or instruments, a simpler technology perhaps of ritual acts, the opening of possibilities in that direction. Let me say something here about experimental poetry: the way we play around to open possibilities or to recover older ones. For myself, I began to write poetry just for the sake of writing and without much further thought about it. I was reading poetry simultaneously; it was an en-terprise, it felt to me, that was very much in the present, as it still feels to me an enterprise very much in the present. But we do, even so, carry a sense of the past with us, so that I found in my own case that the more I got into "experimen-tal" situations with poetry, the more it began to transform my notion of poetry in all times and places. Now the big opening for myself, for people of my generation, was some-time in the 1950s. I'll be talking about this later, this time that was at least the second great eruption in American poetry—the first one coming shortly before the First World War, lasting through the 20s and 30s, seeming to close up in the 40s and part of the 50s when it was smothered by the ris-ing "academics," and then, you know, that closing seeming to allow another outburst, another revolution, another break with what had then become another tyrannizing past, another series of conventions that had built up in the meantime. And when it happened to people like me, it was overwhelming, you know. Suddenly poetry was appearing, which, well, kind of resembled things we had seen in old copies of 1920s, 1930s magazines like *Transition* or in some-thing like the one available book on Dada at that point, the one by Robert Motherwell. The new poetry looked a little bit like that, because in fact it came in something like a straight line from that earlier epoch of experimentation. And it changed, it really changed our whole notion of what a poem could look like. So that you can get faked out, you can open a book—some of the found poetry of Bern Porter is like this—you can open a book and see things there that look like poems, but they're laundry lists, or they're cut-up bits of ads, or pages of mail-order catalogues. Whatever. But in some way they become poems too, particularly, say, the way a really good found-poet like Bern Porter utilizes them.

So, by the time I got around to making *America a Prophecy* with George Quasha, we were able to make a reasonable statement as to how this works. As a kind of opener, though it's out of chronological order, I'll read the part of that statement that seems particularly to pertain to this, this question of the way our image of the poem has changed. [*He reads*:] "Every important change in poetry opens the way for new work in the future and for a redefinition of the past . . ." And of course, we . . . it's very hard writing things together, but we were very careful with the wording: *opens up, opens the way for new work in the future . . .* to put that first, as if to say, we're not engaged here in simply an antiquarian enterprise but one that opens the way for new work in the future *and* for a redefinition of the past. "The 1855 *Leaves of Grass*, for example, is a Declaration of Independence from the 'bondage' "—bondage, that's Whitman's word—"of British and European conventions"—no, it's not Whitman's word, come to think of it, it's Milton's word—"that both heralds the 1950s—Charles Olson's 'projective verse' or Allen Ginsberg's *Howl*—and frees us to see and express the structural particularities of archaic and tribal poetries at a similar remove from those conventions. . . ." Okay, so two things happen. One, Walt Whitman is aware—and this was avant garde, you know, if that term hasn't been too much debased—Walt Whitman was aware of himself as the beginning of something . . . he's constantly proclaiming that . . . he knows there will be new bards after him . . . he seems fairly confident of it: that this is only a beginning. So in

that way he looks into the future, already sets up models for
things that are going to be happening in the future, and also
models to disrupt and fight against, even as, say, somebody
like Pound fights against him. But his work also turns us
back to other possibilities (that's the second thing that happens), points to a phenomenon like Hebrew poetry, the
poetry of the Old Testament, and gives it an equal status
(you know, for people who like to rank things) with poetry
out of the Greek tradition. I wouldn't talk that way myself,
not even when I raise up, say, the image of American Indian
poetry, tribal poetry . . . I mean, it's not a question of
trying to set up new hierarchies: *this is better than that, this
is more important than that* . . . it's not a question of setting
up judgments in that sense. But in a culture where things
have been narrowed down to a single tradition, a single
convention, it's better to assert that this and this are equal,
this and this are possible. So, . . . "all these developments
share the sense of poetry as an act of vision, charged with
the immediate energies of authentic speech and shaped by
its moment in history. Any truly new work, such as that of
Ezra Pound, Gertrude Stein, William Carlos Williams,
Louis Zukofsky, or John Cage, is an invitation to read,
think, and speak differently; it permits a reader (or hearer)
to experience, as nothing else quite does, new 'levels' of
consciousness and verbal meaning. After the Surrealist experiments with 'dream' states, and 'automatic writing,' we
are more attentive to what used to be called the 'irrational.'
Similarly, the efforts of the Dada poets of the 1920s to make
use of 'pure sound' "—a lot of these words are in quotation
marks—"link up in our minds with the wordless poetries of
pre-literate societies (once thought 'meaningless'), the
meditative chants of the East, and certain ritual, magical,
and mystical texts of the West. So, too, the partly or wholly
visual devices of concrete poetry have reminded us that the
separation of the verbal and the pictorial is comparatively
recent; it did not exist for the Egyptians, the Medieval Europeans, or for William Blake. In many such ways—some

subtle, some extreme—the domain of poetry has been extended to include virtually any use of language."

Okay—and with that comes that good slogan of Pound's, "make it new," which is a translation, more or less, from Chinese, from Confucius, the context of which turns up in one of the *Cantos*, if you remember: "Tching prayed on the mountain and/wrote MAKE IT NEW"—big caps—"MAKE IT NEW/on his bath tub/Day by day make it new/cut underbrush/pile the logs/keep it growing." That's as it appears in *Canto* 53.

But just to get off to something that I hope I'll be coming back to later . . . the latest project that I've been working on is "a big Jewish book," a gathering from a tradition in which some of these things are not supposed to occur. [*He picks up a manuscript of* A Big Jewish Book.] So it starts out . . . [*He leafs through to the end.*] 777 manuscript pages . . . it's all planned, I planned it to work out to 777 pages. Not really. But anyway, it starts with a translation by myself and Harris Lenowitz from the Talmud: "Rabbi Eliezer said:/'Prayer *fixed*?/his supplication bears no fruit'/ the question next came up: what/is FIXED? Rabba and Rabbi Yosef answered/'whatever blocks the will/to MAKE IT NEW.' " So at that point, in what appeared to be closed traditions, there was an urge there also towards an open field. In other words, the rabbis there, or Confucius as Pound quotes him, would seem to be talking about the possibilities, the possibilities of renewal, the possibilities of "making it new," the possibilities *not* of a mechanical repetition of things, but of constant invention and re-invention, even if you're working off something as a base, a source—and one way or another we seem always to be working off something as a base, you know . . . although there are other modern poets, even *post*-modern poets, whatever that is, who have opened—well, probably Gertrude Stein as a major example, you know—a kind of poetry in which the past almost disappears, except when Stein or any poet like her chooses to talk about it.

Okay, so there you have it, whatever the source is: the slogan of making it new as applied to that which is old, to that which comes before us, that which is out of the past. And we would find it in other places as well. Charles Olson, for instance. I think at the point he wrote this, twenty years ago, I certainly didn't know about it. 1956. What I did know of Olson then was only as the author of *Call Me Ishmael,* which at first sighting had seemed like a very strange and very wonderful book. That's all I really knew about him then. But he wrote: "We live," he said, "in an age in which inherited literature is being hit from two sides, from contemporary writers who are laying bases of new discourse at the same time that . . . scholars . . . are making available pre-Homeric and pre-Mosaic texts which are themselves eye-openers."[2] I'll get back to that a little bit later, in talking about this book in which I quote him, this book in which I only had a very small part, a book called *Origins: Creation Texts from the Ancient Mediterranean,* translated by Harris Lenowitz and Charles Doria. Of course Olson— this is one of his passionate concerns—was talking about the ancient poetry of the Mediterranean, Babylonian, Egyptian, Sumerian, Canaanite, and so forth. All of that, you know, through translation, through the work of scholars who probably wouldn't have been interested in the enterprise, would even have been hostile to the enterprise as we describe it, which was having the effect of bombarding, of ultimately making it untenable to hold a very narrow, conventional position about poetry. Unless you just wanted to block all of this out of your consciousness—you know, not open up consciousness, not open up possibilities, but instead say, *No, I will continue to go along this conventional way . . . if that other stuff keeps turning up and it bothers me, you know, well, file it away in some specialized area, you know, but the Great Tradition,* as they were calling it then, *the Great Tradition has to remain pure, has to remain untouched.* Or, if you're a little liberal about it, you say, *well, open it up a little bit here and there, you know, but ultimately Babylonia will not regain its position next to Greece and Rome, and if those Jews come in, it's only in that one book, it's just a one time [laughs] single shot book.*

So "being hit from two sides," the experimental poets, "the contemporary writers laying the bases of new discourse," and the scholars who are creating, presenting those "eye-openers," you know . . . but surely not only from the ancient Mediterranean, surely from throughout the world . . . and surely not only from those places, you know, which rose through the creation of city-states and of a political and class network, but also from the pre-political, pre-civilized cultures and traditions! I tried to get at the modern side of it in a book which hasn't circulated much, I wouldn't think, called *Revolution of the Word: A New Gathering of American Avant Garde Poetry 1914-1945.* For more contemporary manifestations (I mean post-World War II), obviously there are many collections . . . well, principally there's still the Donald Allen Anthology, but that's getting a little old, after all. There's *America a Prophecy*, there are the several anthologies of the New York School and related poets. You probably know about most of those anthologies, but in something like this, in *Revolution of the Word*, what I'm trying to do is indicate a continuity of American avant garde concerns going back to, say, the First World War. My own re-education on those matters. And a kind of re-education that I think hasn't gotten into the schools where these things are taught but seems clear to me in the consciousness of many poets working today, certainly poets I know who came through the 50s and 60s.

This is how we were educated and my story is typical. I went into City College of New York in 1948, and I had already by then experienced a kind of first excitement about experimental poetry . . . from books obviously . . . in fact from books that were largely available not in any very erudite setting but in a local public library in the Bronx— near Fordham Road, if any of you know the area. Books by Gertrude Stein, including some of the poetry, Cummings, Joyce, some copies of *Transition, New Directions,* and a little later Pound and so forth. The condition as we went into the universities—and I don't think it's changed tremendously even today—was that some of those names hardly came into the discussion, principally Gertrude Stein, say, or came in very negatively. And this is something that continued to rankle for a long time. Stein was, what, dead two years at this point (she died in '46), and she was still well-known as a figure, as a personality, you know, but there was only one book, if that, being taught then, the *Three Lives*. Otherwise she was dismissed. *That's Gertrude Stein, that's just a one-shot thing, you know, not germinal, not something you can follow . . . that's essentially an eccentric manifestation. Pound, eccentric manifestation. Williams, eccentric manifestation.* So we began to wonder, well, what isn't eccentric? Auden. Auden was the possibility, because he tied in, in a very visible way, you know, with what Eliot and those various critics who were much less than Eliot were putting out, hyping, as a *Great Tradition* . . . but specifically a very narrow English view of things. And a very narrow one, too, because there are a lot of exclusions even on the literary side: the Romantics in particular, or the way that Eliot would down-play Milton, all of that. So there was a constant barrage, a constant coercion toward this narrow point of view that tried to cut us off from what could free us.

So back to 1948 or so. There are still a few figures visible whom we would today recognize as the key modern figures in our terms. Pound is there, Williams is there, but they're viewed, as I said, as early *eccentric* moderns, you know, dead ends . . . *but things will straighten themselves out, things have straightened themselves out.* The straightening (we're told) began in the 1920s, with the so-called "southern fugitives," and it continued up to that point in the 1940s and 50s with (then) younger poets like Wilbur and Lowell, and with people, too, like the very early Merwin, before he went through changes, and so forth. It follows out of the tighter, conventional side of Eliot, and it lays a tremendous emphasis on closure, the return to strict meters. The notion is that the excessive modern thing has played itself out in poetry, that there's now a gradually accelerated pulling

back, a moderating thrust that still retains a kind of
"modern" flourish in the writing. Not everything is lost, but
it's what I've described elsewhere as basically middle ground
modernism, a kind of liberal, reformist movement in poetry
(in other words, and not so secretly, reactionary). And let me
assure you that the poets who some of us have subsequently
come to identify with the 20s and 30s just aren't there. We
begin to pick up—because of the association with Pound,
those of us who become interested in Pound's work—that
there was a poet named Zukofsky, that there was a poet
named Oppen, there was a poet named Bunting . . . and
when they finally begin to reappear in the 1950s, well, it's
interesting how the word does get around: *hey, you know,
Bunting just reappeared* . . . or, when Oppen suddenly
appears with a book: *oh, so that's what happened to Oppen*,
you know, during all of that time. And Reznikoff too . . .
or Walter Lowenfels . . . those people had ceased to exist, they were non-persons. And even lesser-known people,
people even less well-known today, like Harry Crosby, say
. . . a forgotten, marvelous poet. Mina Loy, who Pound
in 1916 was ranking with Marianne Moore . . . she died
in Aspen, oh, probably about six years ago . . . maybe
more than that . . . I don't have the dates very clear—

QUESTION: *Jargon* is publishing a book of hers.

JEROME ROTHENBERG: Yeah, Jonathan Williams, who in
the early, early fifties, middle fifties, put out a selected book
of poems by Mina Loy called *Lunar Baedeker*. It was actually the name of an older book . . . it included the
material from that older book and some more recent work
too. Now Jonathan has been promising a bigger selected
poems of Mina Loy for some time, and hopefully that will
still appear. She's a really terrific poet, very influential
around the time of the First World War . . . in close association with people like Duchamp, who also, in spite of his
great art reputation, still doesn't enter the picture as the important literary influence he was. But Mina Loy . . .
Mina Loy writes one of the great American poems—if it's
American . . . she's actually from England, you know,

but let it pass. . . . She writes, anyway, one of the great contemporary mythic poems, a long and probably uncompleted work called "Anglo Mongrels and the Rose." So maybe that will be reappearing . . . but the point I want to make is that, in spite of things like this, the efforts of Jonathan Williams and others, Crosby and Mina Loy are still, I think, basically forgotten figures. If they're not utterly forgotten at this point, you really can't see very much of the poetry.

Q: Mina Loy gets into many anthologies I've seen.

J.R.: Well, maybe in anthologies of poetry by women. No? Others? I can't think of any really, since the 20s, except my own. [*He holds up copies of* America a Prophecy *and* Revolution of the Word.] She gets into this, I mean; and there have been maybe a couple of other recent attempts at, like, a more modest reassessment, and she may get into those. And Stein has clearly been getting into some more anthologies over the last two years (with some special thanks, again, to the women's movement), and a lot of Stein's work has been independently reissued. Stein is really a monumental 20th-century figure, and I think that's just again becoming evident. With Mina Loy, because she was never *that* well-known, it would be more difficult to get her work back into circulation.

Q: It seems that people like Stein or Crosby regain some reputation through association with historical movements and better known members of their generation.

J.R.: Yeah, Mina Loy too in that sense. Many of us knew of her from stories about that First World War period. In William Carlos Williams' autobiography, for example. Williams was extremely generous in relation to figures like that, though in the fifties even he would seem to have accepted the prevailing literary judgments. And I should mention again, since we're into naming names, someone like Laura Riding . . . although with her the neglect is partly through her own rejection of the whole poetic enterprise.

Who else? Oh, yes. The title of this book I put together about the early avant garde is *Revolution of the Word*, and that was one of the slogans of a very sloganeering poet, Eugene Jolas, who published a magazine, a very important magazine in the 20s and up to the Second World War, named *Transition*. He was himself an interesting poet, though I don't think ultimately of the same stature as Loy or Stein, but he certainly should be remembered more than a lot of other poets who are retained in the standard anthologies. In terms of anything I've done under the heading of so-called "ethnopoetics," Jolas would have to be considered one of the important forerunners, because that was centrally one of the concerns of his magazine, *Transition*. There was one whole issue and parts of others devoted to it.

And there's another slogan [*pointing to the cover of* Revolution of the Word], Mina Loy's from 1914 that I feature here. She got into futurism at that point (movements like that really *move*, in this case from Italy over to the United States), and so she wrote a series called "Futurist Aphorisms," and this is one of them. "Today," she writes, "is the crisis in consciousness." It's a whole consciousness question, as it relates to poetry, and it goes back here to 1914 (and much, much beyond that if we really wanted to take off). Someone, in a description of Stein's work—Mabel Dodge I guess it was—wrote in a special issue of Stieglitz's magazine, *Camera Work*, in which Stein's work first appeared in the United States: "Nearly every thinking person nowadays is in revolt against something, because the craving of the individual is for further consciousness and because consciousness is expanding and is bursting through the moulds that have held it up to now. And so let every man whose private truth is too great for his existing conditions pause before he turn away from Picasso's painting or from Gertrude Stein's writing, for their case is his case."[3] So again, from around the First World War, that proclamation in terms of consciousness. And in the 20s that was carried further . . . not so much this time by the Objectivists, the largely American-Jewish followers of Pound—Oppen, Zukofsky, Reznikoff, Rakosi—who had another field to work. But Crosby is certainly talking about consciousness and Hart

Crane (whom Crosby published and knew) is very much putting an emphasis on it. Also so-called American surrealists like Jolas, Tyler, Ford . . . so that's an important, ongoing development in the 20s and 30s.

If you begin to take all of that into consideration and go by your own sense of descent, then it's not just the "eccentrics," you know, but there's already at this point a *tradition* that we have (it can already be called that) that goes back in a recognizable form to sometime, say, around 1913. That's narrowing it for the moment to America—which is not my ultimate intention. Much more could be said if you took into consideration the whole of the western world and then the whole of the industrializing world, the new communications network being what it is, what it was even then. But just focusing on America, 1913, the events that year are pretty crucial: the Armory Show; a year or so later the arrival of Duchamp in New York; the publication of Stein's *Tender Buttons*; Pound proclaiming Imagism and modifying that more interestingly to Vorticism by maybe the following year. That's all taking place at once. And that last, the Pound thing, is largely under the influence of Italian futurism and of the British cubist painter and novelist Wyndham Lewis . . . and Pound's own devices obviously. Kind of a modified futurism there, in which the contemporary situation is seen as involving the "rush of ideas into the vortex"—the mind, in other words—and poetry becomes a way of dealing with that influx, that proliferation of information that's part of the modern experience, including information about both the present and the past—you know, how do you deal with a mind that's filled in that way, how do you deal with the vortex? So, that's a question that can get a lot of things going, and there were then a lot of questions being raised and shooting off in new directions.

Revolution of the Word was sort of my second take on some of that, focusing on materials that had been left over in effect from *America a Prophecy*, materials from a particular period of time that I thought was really crucial. And one of the regrets I have about *America a Prophecy* is that there was a lack of clear chronological order, 'cause we had been trying the other thing there, the attempt at a synchronous structure; and I thought, you know, as long as it was still current in my mind, that I should try to make a clear statement of where that fit in time-wise. [*He picks up another book.*] Okay, this is Robert Duncan taking a crack at the relation between the new and the old . . . 1967, in *Caterpillar* magazine, an essay called "Rites of Participation," in which he sees our work and striving as a movement towards a new "ideal of vital being"—not like the Greek symposium restricted to a particular aristocracy in a particular place, not the reality of the incomparable nation who raised the incomparable Jehovah in the shape of a man . . . incomparable, single, you know, . . . who gave us *the* Book of capital letters . . . capital Book, capital Vision, single book, single vision . . . but a "symposium of the whole," our "identification with the universe," the bringing up, the raising to consciousness of all that has been "outcast and vagabond . . . the female, the proletariat, the foreign; the animal and vegetative; the unconscious and the unknown; the criminal and failure," to return, "to be admitted, in the creation of what we consider we are." And you can and should add to Duncan's list, so *all* the excluded orders can come together at this point. Because, as someone said, for the first time in many years, many centuries, we can know about some of these things, and perhaps for the first time ever, we can *allow* ourselves to be concerned, to be involved with them, and not so much with what separates us, but increasingly with what connects us with all other orders of human beings, and beyond human beings, with all else in the universe.

Snyder, I think principally in my generation, makes a summary, a kind of great simplification about all this, a simplification which is necessary . . . and he makes it on his own but drawing also on the anthropology, as it turns out, of Stanley Diamond, in case you want to follow up on that, to see the roots of that in research, so to speak. "My own opinion," Snyder says, and this is in capsule his special view of history, "My own opinion is that we are now experiencing a surfacing (in a specifically 'American' incarnation) of the Great Subculture which goes back as far perhaps as the late Paleolithic"—it's great . . . the GSC, you know . . . like the Gross National Product, GNP or something . . . the Great Sub-Culture—"which goes back as far perhaps as the late Paleolithic. This subculture of illuminati has been a powerful undercurrent in all higher civilizations. In China it manifested as Taoism, not only Lao-tzu but the Yellow Turban revolt and medieval Taoist secret societies; and the Zen Buddhists up till early Sung. Within Islam the Sufis; in India the various threads converged to produce Tantrism. In the West it has been represented largely by a string of heresies starting with the Gnostics, and on the folk level by 'witchcraft.' " So, if I can take that, without going further into it, and can translate it in terms of poetry, as presumably Snyder would too, then I would say that the origin of poetry, the *mainstream* of poetry to be exact, goes back to the old tribes and has been carried forward by the great subterranean culture, the great subculture, as a kind of basic and historical poetic process.

Q: It's Robert Duncan's notion that "tradition" provides us with a sort of "permission" to extend the poetic act, a license to "set out for ourselves."

J.R.: Yeah, I think Duncan goes back and forth as to whether he really needs permission or not. You know, clearly Duncan would do it without permission . . . you know, *may I leave the room?* [*Laughter.*] I mean, for someone with that old anarchistic streak, to have to always first be told! And I think too that there's a normal impulse to know where we are in time and space and not to take anybody else's word for it. So to my mind this subculture thing presents certain clarifications, although it is, as I say, a simplification, to which people can raise historical objections and so on, but in the end I think it holds. It's a working view of history, and I don't think it's a false view. And I think you can see it borne out too when looking back to those early written works with which presumably we're all familiar. So, for example, in one of Diamond's very good essays, "Plato and the Idea of the Primitive," he takes the tenth chapter of *The Republic*, takes Plato at his word there, and says, people have always wondered, I mean, *does he really want to banish the poets? You can't mean it, can you, Plato?* You know, Ginsberg was telling a story about when he was in Cuba, and the guardians of the state came and, well, they kidnapped him and sent him out of the country. *Me? Hey, Plato, you mean me? You mean you're gonna banish ME from the Republic?* So, when I used to read Plato, I really wasn't sure, you know . . . did he mean it? Well, it turns out that he meant it . . . and Diamond is very good because he can point out, well, what poets is he talking about exactly? And from Plato's own description it's clear that it's those poets, the real poets, who are coming out of a shamanistic tradition, you know—let's use that term, a shamanistic tradition—that's tribal and in conflict, clearly in conflict with the city-state, with the political state as it's developing in Greece. The poets, as Plato indicates, are those who play with, who allow contradiction, which he cannot tolerate. I mean, he's one of the first to come along and to say, at least at that point, that contradiction is very bad, it's a lie . . . and the truth ultimately has something to do with the annihilation of contradiction . . . the truth has to be self-consistent. Well, the poets are not self-consistent, you know, they tell lies all the time; and for telling those lies they have to be banished from any kind of rational fascistic republic . . . or communistic republic . . . but not really communistic at all, because ultimately the sin there is, if not communism, at least communalism. And, you know, if you study back into the attempt to annihilate the tribes of North America, say, one of the things that was constantly being said against them was that they were "Communists." My wife, Diane Rothenberg, is doing a massive research project on what happened to the Seneca Indians around the year 1800, and one of the standard white attacks was that the Indians would never "achieve" to civilization until they ceased to be communists. So, Plato finally says, *no, if you think I mean a complete banishment of the poets, that's not exactly it. I used to be a poet myself,* he says, *and I don't really mean that. I mean that we should permit those poets to remain in the Republic who*—what's the phrase?—*sing hymns to the gods and the praises of great men.* So, if you want to be welcome in the Republic, you know, that's ultimately the message. *Stay good. Stay clean.* You can even write very pretty poetry sometimes, if you do it right. I was down in Cuba, as a case in point, where they tell you that of course it's possible to do such things as concrete poetry down there. They tell you that and at the same time they're carrying Ginsberg off, or rounding up the homosexuals, or rounding up the hippies or putting poets under the gun, you know, who dare to speak sarcastically about Fidel—that which should be the poet's one great right, our heritage from ancient sacred clownhood. So you ask about it and they tell you *but our poets also write concrete poetry* . . . which is an improvement you know, a marked improvement over the Russian situation, where "our poets" don't even write concrete poetry, except secretly.

Okay . . . other sources as well, feeding into this. As I said before, I'm concentrating on American figures and American contemporaries, and I'm playing very lightly, or by-passing entirely what are important fundamental movements, like French Surrealism and Dadaism, and so forth. There the opening into and redefinition of the past was also very clearly seen—particularly, say, for the Surrealists and the program they set themselves of dreaming back to the primitive "dream-time," and through the dream of closing up and bringing together all times and places. The French and Spanish were much stronger on that till very recently, but what the American poetics has now done in a very special way is to take that dream-time and put it into association with history per se. I gather Ed Sanders was talking about some of this last year, the piece that appeared in *Loka,* the poet as investigator . . . yeah, a big emphasis on history there, that goes along with a concern with history

and geography, as in the work of, just to single out two figures, Pound and Olson. Pound again . . . some of his best
statements are extremely simple, like the definition of the
"epic" as "a poem including history," which opens up into a
great deal more. So, a reconsideration of time and place,
chronos, topos. And it's this that permits us to look back,
makes it possible for us to see this kind of new and old
poetics in descriptions of systems like Tantra, Kabbalah,
Gnosis, American Indian vision gathering, and so on. And
before people were talking too much of that, there was very
acutely the thrill of recognition in picking up a book on
Tantric art, say, or Gershom Scholem's book on . . . what
was the first book called? *Major Trends in Jewish Mysticism*
. . . to see in so much that Scholem is describing—the
mystical work, the so-called "Path of the Names" of a figure
like Abraham Abulafia—processes which were already under
way among us. So if you read, for example, Jackson Mac
Low's description of how he comes into chance poetics, it's
not only through John Cage, it's also through Gershom
Scholem and Abraham Abulafia. And that's no trivial thing.
It's interesting, as it's interesting also to be able to turn back
now to works like Freud's *Interpretation of Dreams* . . .
something I did just recently because I was working on the
big Jewish book . . . and Stein said the first way of recognizing a poem was visually, so I opened up Freud's *Interpretation of Dreams* . . . I was looking for quotes, you know,
because the big Jewish book is the kind of anthology where
I also do a lot of quoting . . . so I opened it up, and these
prose-poems began appearing there. They were descriptions
of dreams, and set on the page as they were, indented, with
space before and after, they looked very clearly like prose-
poems. So I started to read them and, you know, they even
read like prose-poems: Freud read like a hard-line French
surrealist dream-time prose-poem writer. And it suddenly
occurred to me (because I'm always being startled by
truisms) that Freud is the influence, the creator there, because he's doing those poems in the 1890s, inventing a structure for Jacob or Breton to follow. And what he's saying

about dreams uses terminology that's familiar from at least one area of contemporary poetics, involving transformations and the relation of opposites, so this could literally be a text on poetics. But then you realize too that Freud really knows this, that he even gives some of the dreams titles, makes them titled works. And the thing that clinched it for me is that he's got one he calls "A Beautiful Dream." It's one of his patient's dreams, which wasn't, I don't think, beautiful in the trite, pretty image sense but because the structure was tremendous, complex . . . the dream structure . . . and then to top it off he calls that whole process of dreaming, the "Dream Work," because he sees it, or we do through him, as a creative process. *The Dream Work.*

Q: There is a connection, if you read the work of Geza Roheim, between poetry and the language of schizophrenics, as well as between poetry and the archetypes of C.G. Jung.

J.R.: Yeah, well, there are a couple of instances in here [*he shows a copy of* America a Prophecy] where we presented schizophrenic uses of language that one recognizes as part of, or related to, poetic process. It's even possible, we go on to say, to view all that as a strategy—although a failed one—to push toward vision, illumination, in an age cut-off from it. And Roheim is important for us because he's one of the major writers on the Australian aborigine "dream-time." So at the time I was founding *Alcheringa*,⁴ I was mainly drawing the name and the idea round it from Roheim, the way it turns up in his book, *Eternal Ones of the Dream. Alcheringa*, anyway, is an Australian aboriginal word whose literal meaning is dream-time, but it's hard to define . . . Roheim's "eternal ones of the dream" in one instance, Freud's "dream work" in another. Obviously you also pick up a poetics, the presence of a poetics, in Jung but there I think it's quite self-conscious, really literary. In his book, *The Truth of Life and Myth*, Duncan makes the interesting comment that Jung is almost too smooth, too refined, that Freud is the real gutsy one. Duncan has a very ambiguous relation to theosophy and so forth, and he says, having grown up with such high-minded symbols, that Jung comes on too much like one of Duncan's aunts, say, because Duncan grew up in that kind of family. Freud comes on like my grandmother . . . the one in our family who knew the words for things, what Duncan calls the myths, the "lowness of the story." And, if anything, Freud makes the dreams more gutsy than they seem at surface. I mean, it's not polished up and the degree of symbolization isn't as sophisticated, but you're really simply into the whole uncomfortable dreaming process . . . terrifying dreams, sheer terror . . . it doesn't turn out to be something better, prettier, all beauty and refinement. It's scary, right, and if it's scary, then it's really scary. Really *dirty* dreams.

Okay. A kind of poetics turns up also in the philosophy of someone like Wittgenstein, say, who's obviously also been a contemporary influence, where, for example, he describes philosophy as a "fight against the fascination which forms of expression exert upon us." He's defining philosophy, and in a certain way it hold for poetry as well, because that old dichotomy, that split that Plato made from the other side, may be behind us. So poetry might also, in some of its forms, be seen as a "fight against the fascination which forms of expression exert upon us." In that sense, the work, the poetic work, becomes a questioning of assumptions. Again, going back to that idea of the freedom of the imagination that I spoke of earlier—the poetic liberty, the poet's traditional privilege—let me put it into a context again where it's not familiar. [*He picks up the manuscript of* A Big Jewish Book.] This is to quote from a putative ancestor of mine, Rabbi Meier of Rothenberg, who was a great Talmudist as I understand it, and the author of many *responsa*, answers to questions about tradition and law; so they asked him at one time—never mind the technicalities of this, it's really the answer that counts—they said, "Is not the liturgical poet who first writes that clay vessels in which leaven was cooked must be broken before Passover and then states that they may be stored away in wooden sheds, guilty of a contradiction?" And Rabbi Meier of Rothenberg answers. "It is poetic liberty to state together two contradictory propositions."

That's his entire answer. He doesn't then go on to say, *but we must banish the poets from the ghetto*, or wherever we were at that point in time. It is simply, in other words, that there's a function of poetry that allows it, that says there has to be that area of free play . . . and poets of course want more and more of it, to open up the world. So, then, a questioning of assumptions.

Well, at a certain point I became—again not individually; I was *one of those* who became interested in questioning the link between poetry and writing, who spoke in terms of a return to the "oral bases" of poetry, so that poetry was not to be defined as principally a form of writing. Poetry is a process of language and of mind, and ultimately, in an age of writing, writing is one of the ways in which poetry manifests itself. Then, too, I was questioning the poetry and civilization link, and the "civilized" view of poetry as an effort largely rational, conventional, and closed. That kind of assumption becomes open to question, but so does the counter-view if fetishized into the only truth. So the first step was not to set the primitive/tribal/oral over the other, but to think of it as prior or equal, necessary to whatever kind of future work it is we're doing. And the first book in which I was able to make any moves in that direction was *Technicians of the Sacred*, which came out, I think, in 1967; and there the question for me, once I had been a while with some of this material, was how to break or alter the dominance of the literal, civilized culture over our poetics. In other words, the effort by then was to bring in the primitive, the tribal, the oral, and to try to see the ways in which it's manifested itself in many times and places. That was the first part of it: a mapping, an attempt at a mapping, the beginning of a mapping, a personal mapping of the primitive and the oral. And the second was to work by analogies to the present situation, to the way in which our poetics, our poetry, is being made at this time. Those of you who have read *Technicians* will see, at one point in the introduction, the way I attempted to set it out, again simplifying, in two columns: one, things that are going on at the present time;

two, primitive forms, primitive ideas, attitudes in other cultures, and so forth, that resemble those.

What I want to do next time we meet is to concentrate on the new work that I've been into along these lines, that is, the big Jewish book I've been referring to, which is simply going to be called *A Big Jewish Book*, 'cause I want to avoid poetic titles for that one, and subtitled "poems and other visions of the Jews from tribal times to present" . . . from about the tenth century B.C. to the 1970s. I had also wanted to go through these various anthologies, these assemblages, and tell you what I was attempting to do in each of them. And particularly in relation to *Shaking the Pumpkin*, I wanted and still may try to concentrate on questions of translation, in so far as translation of this poetry involves chanting, and to see what's involved in translating a distinctively different language and culture and what seems to be a fundamentally different poetic set. What, for example, do you do in situations where the original not only uses words in the way we do in conventional western poetry, but also incorporates so-called meaningless syllables, distorts words from their spoken form, goes through various changes that are normally ignored in the process of translation? And if you're translating from a chanted poetry, is there a way of bringing the chant across into the new work? Is this, then, a process of composition rather than simply a process of translation? So maybe if the time works out right, I can get from the question of modern and tribal analogues (which I started on before) to that of translation as composition.

In doing *Technicians* it did seem to me that the analogies were important, to let us see this work not only in distant or even antiquarian terms, but in so far as intersections already existed with contemporary work, work being done by the mid-1960s when I was mapping this out. A question that came up then was whether the contemporary work was simply, you know, coincidentally analogous, structurally analogous for whatever reasons, or whether there was some kind of steady, direct influence. So, if I can just move into the

1970s and offer Anne Waldman's work *Fast Speaking Woman*, as an example. My first take on that, if I didn't know anything else, would be that what she's doing is analogous to certain kinds of chanting, certain repetitive patterns that are fairly widespread in tribal and oral poetry. But I realize also that with that poem, she's picking up from a specific tradition, which she gets through translation, and through a recording in fact . . . [*to Anne Waldman*] I mean, you've heard the Wasson recording of the Mexican shamaness Maria Sabina? The words are so close it's almost like an extended translation. So, both analogy and influence are operative, or for an early example, check out the work of Tristan Tzara, which I only touched on very lightly in *Technicians of the Sacred*, because I didn't know much about it at the time—what Tzara does with African and Pacific Island poetry. I knew when I was into *Technicians* that the Dadaists had had a sense of what they called *poesie nègre*—you know, *nigger* poetry, *black* poetry—but I didn't truly know in what sense they were using the term. You know, they would get up at public performances and would do some kind of Dadaist equivalent to what they took to be African chanting. And Tzara, of all the Dadaists, seemed to be the one principally involved in this and at one point was supposed to be assembling a book of translations, workings, called *Poemes Nègres*, but the book never came out. So I wondered, is there a steady line of transmission among the surrealists and so on, and was Tzara really presenting anything, even by bad translation, to the people that he was hanging out with? But I didn't have any of his African material to look at until last year, when the first volume of what's going to be the complete works of Tristan Tzara came out in French; and in it, partly reconstructed by the editor, were the Negro poems, the African poems. So, because I was editing *Alcheringa* magazine and we had a lot of space, I got Pierre Joris, whose first languages in fact are French and German, to do a complete translation into English of the Tzara originals, because I thought it would be useful, you know, to see Tzara for the first time as a direct link. He's right in the center of the surrealist movement, and the question is, were the surrealists (who spoke so much about it) being *directly* influenced, or did they just think that they were being influenced? Was it just a vague idea, a *completely* vague idea of African, tribal poetry, sort of a spin-off from what they knew already, what they had all seen of tribal art and heard of tribal music? But Tzara in fact was acting in a much more direct way as a transmitter. That's important to me not just for the historical record but more personally—because it showed again (as did conversations with many of my immediate contemporaries) that I wasn't the only one (although I felt independent, even isolated, at the time) but that it was part of the condition of being alive in this century, speaking for more than myself as a poet . . .

All of this helps me to understand the kind of excitement that I myself was picking up when I was in graduate school back in 1952 at the University of Michigan and was wandering through, was finally permitted to wander through the stacks of a big library, and coming on poetry in other than the literature sections—the sections, in other words, devoted principally to anthropology. There were these great poetic works there that had been put out earlier in the century by the Bureau of American Ethnology and various institutions under a number of different ethnographic imprints. So it was a true excitement, to immediately open up those books and, even in what were often poor translations, clumsy, anthropologist translations, to come on something that was very real and very genuine. So, for example, when I was reading, then or later, a book by Marius Barbeau on the Indians of the Pacific Northwest, I found a description by a Gitksan Indian named Isaac Tens, of how he became a shaman . . . and he was describing an overwhelming, strange experience—unsought, uncalled for in his case [*skimming* Technicians]: how he was wandering through the woods when suddenly the mystic animals appeared to him . . . and they were bringing songs with them . . . and he was in a trance . . . he fell unconscious, he was

bleeding from his nose, he managed to wake up, his head
was buried in a snow bank, he made his way back to the village . . . and the older shamans recognizing what was
happening, began to gather around him to support him, to
work with him. "My flesh seemed to be boiling," he says,
"my body was quivering. While I remained in this state, I
began to sing. A chant was coming out of me without my
being able to do anything to stop it. Many things appeared
to me presently: huge birds and other animals . . . these
were visible only to me, not to the others in my house. Such
visions happen when a man is about to become a shaman;
they occur of their own accord. The songs force themselves
out complete without any attempt to compose them. But I
learned and memorized those songs by repeating them."

This is a very interesting statement and, if you want to
put it in those terms, it's an especially interesting statement
about poetics, the process of poem-making or song-making.
*The songs force themselves out complete without any at-
tempt to compose them.* I mean, I assume you've been hearing a lot of talk in these precincts about that kind of
composition; and when I read that or similar accounts (but I
think it was specifically this Isaac Tens piece, which is so
clearly stated), oh, you know, it tied up so much with the
idea of immediate spontaneous composition. I don't tend to
work precisely in those terms, except for that whole mystery
of composition in which poems do happen. I mean, you
never know when the thing will come out whole and
complete, and the choicest poetry, after all, is the poetry
that does emerge in that way, although you learn, as the
shamans did also, techniques for working, for getting yourself into a condition where poetry may happen.

But reading Tens, anyway, there were things that immediately sprang into mind: Shelley's description (it's part of
Romanticism's gift to us), Shelley's description of the terror
of initial inspiration and composition; Whitman and "Out
of the Cradle Endlessly Rocking," which I take in some
sense to be an actual description, an actual experience,
where, like with Tens, it's through a totem-like animal, a

mystic animal, the two birds of the poem, that he starts to "see." He tends to sentimentalize it of course: the one bird disappears, the other bird is singing and weeping for his lost mate. Isaac Tens didn't have to project like that, you know; he didn't have to sentimentalize his totem in order to start to feel. But still it seems to me something very similar was happening for both of them. Whitman is the boy, the poet, and this is an initiation experience, like Tens' initiation into vision, from which comes, Whitman says, "all songs, all melodies," all opening up for him.

And along with that, I presented in *Technicians* (among the possible examples) Ginsberg's description of his vision of Blake in the tenement in Harlem, which was also a kind of call to poetry. I would assume he had, in some sense, heard the call before, but that solidified it, that made it real, and it fits into a whole tradition, you know, from the shamans and after the shamans . . . a tradition one can trace through those parts of the mystical literature that are not only a history of mysticism per se, but a history of poesis. At points those seem to be very close, and at points they obviously separate, and one doesn't want to confuse the two processes, mysticism and *poesis*, as a single process unless it becomes quite clear, you know, that they are in fact a single process.

Okay. I should come back here to the sound poems. And there, it seemed to me at first, that the Dadists had invented this in their own terms, but then I wondered, had they *re*-invented it, you know, because Tristan Tzara was there, and one of the "sound poems" that Tristan Tzara read at the Cabaret Voltaire was a transcription, simply a transliteration of a Maori poem from New Zealand . . . not translated, just whatever he could make out of those sounds. And the Dadaists knew as well that there were in fact tribal "sound poems." Maybe not all the Dadaists knew it; maybe when Hugo Ball says, as I quote him in *Technicians*, "The other night I invented a new form of poetry without words which I will call *lautgedichte*," sound poetry, maybe he isn't aware that this has happened at other times, other places. I don't know. But I do know that once you become aware of the contemporary sound poetry and you look back at the past, you will find poems without words, structures without words, that resemble poetry. And that may start you making them yourself—as it did with me, for any of you who know the "Horse-Song" and my other sound-works. The present changing the past and vice versa. The same for visual poems, or visual structures we now read as poems: you know, if this is a poem here, then in a sense it's a poem there, which is disguising for a moment the question of function, that sound and visual "poems" may "here" and "there" have different uses. But in other instances, the matter of function is precisely what ties the tribal to the modern: Isaac Tens to Walt Whitman, or to Shelley, or to Ginsberg and myself and so many others. I mean, it is a *visionary function* throughout all that.

But let me give another instance, a poem I would not have left out under any circumstances: the translation of a Navajo poem, which will lead into my own work later on. "War God's Horse Song," as it's titled here . . . an earlier translation of it. [*Reading from* Technicians of the Sacred:] "I am the Turquoise Woman's son / On top of Belted Mountain / beautiful horses—slim like a weasel! / My horse with a hoof like a striped agate, / with his fetlock like a fine eagle plume: / my horse whose legs are like quick lightning / whose body is an eagle-plumed arrow: / my horse whose tail is like a trailing black cloud. / The Little Holy Wind blows thru his hair. / My horse with a mane made of short rainbows. / My horse with ears made of round corn. / My horse with eyes made of big stars. / My horse with a head made of mixed waters. / My horse with teeth made of white shell. / The long rainbow is in his mouth for a bridle / and with it I guide him. / When my horse neighs, different-colored sheep follow. / I am wealthy because of him . . ." And then the ending, which you've probably heard in many other places: "Before me peaceful / Behind me peaceful / Under me peaceful. / Over me peaceful— / Peaceful voice when he neighs. / I am everlasting and peaceful. / I stand for my horse." I had come across this in a book by Dane and Mary Roberts Coolidge on the Navajos—"my horse with a hoof like a striped agate, with a fetlock like a fine eagle plume, my horse's legs like quick lightning. . . ." That kind of pattern—at the same time that I was reading, in David Antin's translation, Andre Breton's great Surrealist poem, "Free Union": "My wife whose hair is a brush fire / Whose thoughts are summer lightning / Whose waist is an hourglass / Whose waist is the waist of an otter caught in the teeth of a tiger / Whose mouth is a bright cockade with the fragrance of a star of the first magnitude . . ." And so forth and so on. I think that, in any case, I would have been struck by the "War God's Horse Song," but the two were in fact converging, and that brought a recognition of both affinities and influence: that Breton had been in the United States during the Second World War and had lived for sometime in Arizona. He's supposed to have had, for whatever it means, a tremendous kachina doll collection, presumably the best in France. It was a central Surrealist concern.

Q: It has been said that the Hopi "sound poem" in *America a Prophecy* may have been used to "name" locations the ancestral beings stopped at in the time of the first migrations.

J.R.: Well, you're conjecturing on that as one possibility. Maybe everybody conjectures about these poems, including many Indians. The feeling is that they have no translatable words and yet they do have meaning; that is, they're full of meaning . . . they're meaning-full and they're old and where did they come from, but what then is the language of the poems? And you get various takes on that. So, it's an old forgotten language, some say, or it's a mapping device, or it's the language of the gods.

Q: Can the origins of that poem be traced? The specificity of the sounds are they particular to certain languages and cultures?

J.R.: Well, what's clear I suppose is that that poem is Hopi, as some other poem is Navajo, some other poem is Seneca, and so on. And yet the words are . . . rather, the sounds, the sounds are like words, they seem to be a language, they seem to be from some language.

I became very interested in that aspect, specifically, of American Indian poetry, and when I was doing the next book, *Shaking the Pumpkin*, I got deeply involved in the whole translation question. I had been much freer and easier in *Technicians of the Sacred*, where mostly I was going for older translations, translations from scholarly anthropological sources. People think there's a lot of rewriting involved in what I put together, but truly I don't think there ever was that much, you know—just enough, but not *that* much. I mean, my intention in most cases was not to significantly change the original but to make it more immediate as a reading or hearing experience.

During the break between those two books I became more directly involved in the translation process, even attempting to get closer to the source. The rattle poem that I started this session with would be a good example. If you know *Shaking the Pumpkin*, it's one of those pieces early in the book that look like concrete poems though, of course, they're "songs." The idea there was that the particular strength of Seneca song-poetry was that it used very few words; it wasn't to be scorned on that basis but could rather be seen as a kind of Seneca "minimal poetry." That was a usable term, a viable term that related it to something like minimal art and poetry, as one spoke about it in the 1960s. So here, I could say, is a traditional minimal poetry, and that is a matter of some sophistication. There is no point to saying, out of context, that because there are so few words used here, this is a really primitive piece . . . I mean, *they just couldn't get it up to get a lot of words into the poem!* But that's to miss the development here of a "minimal poetry," and to get that development across, to translate it, I presented it on the page in terms of another kind of minimal poetry, you know, the way it turns up in contemporary concrete works. Even there, I wasn't minimal enough. I would do it a little differently now.

Anyway, the title line here:

T

h

e   H E H E H H E H

                                        H E H E H H E H

The animals are coming by   H E H U H H E H

n   H E H E H H E H

i   H E H E H H E H

m

a

l

s

. . . is really the meaningful part of the song, the translatable part: "the animals are coming." And with that come some syllables, *heh, heh, heh* . . . right? The poem on the page is a kind of simplification of what's actually being sung . . . and it's set up in five lines because it's repeated five times in the singing. But in the very center, instead of an *eh* sound, I put in an *uh*, you know, as a kind of [*exhaling heavily*] *uhh, unk, uhh*, sound, which was a way of trying to indicate the *uhhhhhh*, the expulsion of the breath at the end of that piece. I mapped all of that out, although it doesn't teach you how to sing it. . . . I mean, I'm not transcribing in that sense, but I am, you know, mapping out all of the elements.

So, those are the elements of the original poem as I understand it, and they're flattened out and presented as a kind of visual, concrete poetry. Then later, later on, I found that I could go back and sing those songs. That was another

approach to it. Well, at the same time I was doing these
Seneca poems, I was collaborating on a second series, from
Navajo, with the ethnomusicologist, David McAllester,
who's at Wesleyan University. We had been introduced, I
think, by Richard Grossinger, and we got into a discussion
of that "War God's Horse Song" that I just read to you in
relation to Breton's poem—the description of the horse—and
I said, "Boy, I would love to, I'd love to translate that.
That's a wonderful, you know, a knockout poem—and by no
means 'minimal.' But I'm interested to know, too, is
Collidge's translation the way it goes in the Navajo, or is
this one of those instances in which there are also many
'meaningless' syllables," and so forth. And McAllester indi-
cated, in fact, that that was not the way it went in Navajo
. . . and, yes, there were many meaningless syllables. So
we worked together towards another kind of translation, a
"total translation" of the sound that carried through six of
the seventeen horse songs he had collected—really three
pairs of two horse songs each three shifts of melody, with a
lot of repetitions of the same element from song to song. I
had never sung before that, and I didn't anticipate that I
would end up singing the songs. Well, maybe I had a suspi-
cion in the back of my mind, but it didn't seem reasonable,
because I was never able to carry a tune, so. . . . What I
wanted was something that you only get after a process of
composition. I've got a greed for poems, and I suppose, once
I was into it, I wanted songs. I didn't want to carry off, to rip
off the Navajo songs (as the accusation sometimes goes), and
I didn't anyway think I would really be able to sing them.
On the other hand, I did want to give the immediate sense
of what goes on in that kind of Navajo poem. And that
meant translation as I had never done it before: translation
so literal to the sound, so total, that it changes everything—
the words, the vocables, the music—and yet stays very close.
I've written about it elsewhere—as a process of both translation and composition—but the best way to show it is by
singing.[5] [*After some explanation, he sings the "10th
Horse Song of Frank Mitchell," to end the lecture.*]

Notes

1. A series of anthologies edited or co-edited by Jerome Rothenberg between 1968 and the present: *Technicians of the Sacred, Shaking the Pumpkin, America a Prophecy* (with George Quasha), *Revolution of the Word, A Big Jewish Book* (in manuscript), and *Origins* (edited by Harris Lenowitz and Charles Doria, for which Jerome Rothenberg did the preface). See Sources for full bibliographical information.

2. Quoted in Lenowitz and Doria, *Origins,* see Sources, page xiii.

3. Quoted in Rothenberg, *Revolution of the Word,* see Sources, page 89.

4. *Alcheringa: Ethnopoetics,* described by the editors as "a first magazine of the world's tribal poetries," was founded by Jerome Rothenberg, with Dennis Tedlock, in 1971. The first five issues were printed independently, and those following, as a part of Boston University Publications. Jerome Rothenberg withdrew after volume 3, number 1 of the "new series" to pursue "a broader range of interests than there possible," as editor of *New Wilderness Letter,* etc.

5. Versions of some of the *Horse Songs* appear in *Shaking the Pumpkin* (see Sources and in Jerome Rothenberg's *Poems for the Game of Silence* [New Directions, 1975]). The fullest description is in his essay, "Total Translation," first published in George Quasha's magazine, *Stony Brook,* and reprinted in Abraham Chapman, *Literature of the American Indians,* New American Library, 1975. Recorded performances have been published in Jerome Rothenberg, *Horse Songs & Other Soundings* (S-Press Tonbandverlag, Germany, 1975) and *6 Horse Songs for 4 Voices* (New Wilderness Audiographics, New York, 1977: multi-track cassette).

Sources

ALLEN, DONALD M., *The New American Poetry* (New York: Grove Press, 1960).

ANTIN, DAVID, "Some Versions of André Breton," in *Poems from the Floating World,* ed. Jerome Rothenberg (New York: Hawk's Well Press, 1962), vol. 4, p. 7.

BARBEAU, MARIUS, *Medicine-Men on the North Pacific Coast* (Ottawa: National Museum of Canada Bulletin, No. 152, 1958).

COOLIDGE, DANE and MARY ROBERTS, *The Navajo Indians* (Boston: Houghton Mifflin, 1930), p. 2.

DIAMOND, STANLEY, "Plato & the Definition of the Primitive," in S. Diamond, *In Search of the Primitive* (New Brunswick, N.J.: Transaction Books, 1974), p. 176.

DUNCAN, ROBERT, "Rites of Participation," in Clayton Eshlemen, *A Caterpillar Anthology* (New York: Anchor Books, 1971), p. 23.

————, *Truth of Life & Myth* (Fremont, Michigan: Sumac Books, 1968).

FREUD, SIGMUND, "The Interpretation of Dreams" [*Die Traumdeutung*] (New York: Avon Books, 1965).

LENOWITZ, HARRIA and DORIA, CHARLES, *Origins: Creation Texts from the Ancient Mediterranean* (New York: Anchor Books, 1975).

LOY, MINA, *Lunar Baedeker* (Highlands, N.C.: Jargon Books, 1958).

MOTHERWELL, ROBERT, *The Dada Painters & Poets* (New York: Wittenborn, Schultz, Inc., 1951).

OLSON, CHARLES, *Human Universe & Other Essays* (New York: Grove Press, 1967).

POUND, EZRA, *The Cantos of Ezra Pound* (New York: New Directions, 1970).

RÓHEIM, GÉZA, *The Eternal Ones of the Dream* (New York: International Universities Press, 1945).

ROTHENBERG, JEROME, *Technicians of the Sacred* (New York: Doubleday & Comp., 1968).

————, *Shaking the Pumpkin: Traditional Poetry of the Indian North Americas* (New York: Doubleday & Comp., 1972).

———— and QUASHA, GEORGE, *America a Prophecy: A New Reading of American Poetry from Pre-Columbian Times to the Present* (New York: Random House, Vintage Books, 1974).

————, *Revolution of the Word: A New Gathering of American Avant Garde Poetry 1914-1945* (New York: Seabury Press, 1974).

————, *A Big Jewish Book: Poems & Other Visions of the Jews from Tribal Times to Present* (New York: Doubleday & Comp., 1978).

SANDERS, ED, "Investigative Poetry," in *Loka 2: A Journal from Naropa Institute,* ed. Rick Fields (New York, Anchor Books, 1976).

SCHOLEM, GERSHOM, *Major Trends in Jewish Mysticism* (New York: Schocken Books, 1946).

SNYDER, GARY, "Passage to More than India," in G. Snyder, *Earth House Hold* (New York: New Directions, 1969).

WALDMAN, ANNE, *Fast Speaking Woman* (San Francisco: City Lights, 1975).

WITTGENSTEIN, LUDWIG VON, *The Blue & Brown Books* (New York: Harper & Brothers, 1958), p. 27.

WHITMAN, WALT, "Out of the Cradle Endlessly Rocking," from W. Whitman, *Leaves of Grass* (New York: Norton & Comp., 1965), pp. 246-253.

Photo by Rachel Homer

Anne Waldman

MY LIFE A LIST

JULY 29, 1976

I'VE BEEN ASKED with increasing frequency by students here
how I became a poet—what were the antecedents, who came
before, how I've changed, and what I've written since I was
a student myself. So today, I would like to talk about my
own background as a poet, influences, life situations, and so
on. And I would like to read a few early works and talk
about the circumstances surrounding the writing of them, as
well as about the notion of community in the late sixties
and early seventies as related to the history of the Poetry
Project at St. Mark's Church-in-the-Bowery in New York
City. My own changes paralleled those of many poets at the
time, and for that reason, in their own modest way, can be
termed as history. . . .

I had a fortunate childhood, I guess, in that my parents
were both writers of sorts. My father was a hack writer for a
magazine called *Why?*—a bit like the magazine *Pageant*—
writing articles on drugs, how to stop smoking and the like,
so there was an aura about the house of writing for professional purposes. Yellow copy paper, carbons, typewriter rib-
bons, sharpened blue and red pencils: I loved the smell of
those things. He was also going to college on the GI Bill,
after the war, so as I was a child he was a student—prin-

cipally studying literature, writing, journalism. He became
a speed reading expert, and I was his guinea pig and encouraged to read voraciously. I could read a hundred pages of
Thomas Wolfe an hour. Later, I realized that one could
never read poetry this way. It really slowed me down: a
much different experience.

My mother, on the other hand, had lived for a number of
years in Greece, having gone over when she was nineteen
years old upon marrying the son of the Greek poet, Anghelos
Sikelianos. She had done translations of Sikelianos' work and
had been involved in the recreation of the ancient Greek
festivals in Delphi instigated by her energetic mother-in-law,
Eva Palmer Sikelianos. So, she knew modern Greek fluently,
some ancient Greek, and also French, and was basically a
self-educated woman who loved poetry. Poetry was the food
in her life, and I think some of that enthusiasm was passed
onto me: something about the experience of poetry being es-
sential, like food and light. So, at an early age poetry was
one of the biggest "highs" for me, or something like that.

And then I had some seminal experiences in high school,
particularly through one English teacher, Jon Beck Shank, a
real aesthete who loved Wallace Stevens' poetry and would
simply come to class and read Stevens' work aloud. And you
know Stevens is so mysterious, abstract, cerebral, and
musical, funny, too—all those things—and hearing the music
of it, having it just roll over you so you could make your
own conclusions, rather than having to analyze it to death—
although we'd do some of that too—was a real treat. I literally remember getting chills with the repetition of the
pronoun "she," in *The Idea of Order at Key West*. All his
Florida tropical poems are wonderful. Like William Carlos
Williams, there are people actually talking in Stevens' poems.
I loved *The River-Merchant's Wife: A Letter,* Pound's poem
after Rihaku. It really appeals to a romantic teenager's
sensibility: "At fifteen I stopped scowling,/I desired my dust
to be mingled with yours/Forever and forever and forever./Why should I climb the lookout?" Jonathan Cott—the
poet and journalist—one of my best friends in high school

turned me on to a lot of poets, notably Rilke, and we constantly showed each other our own works. And, of course, there was my parents' library and the Eighth Street Bookshop up the street; I grew up on Macdougal Street in Greenwich Village. The Don Allen Anthology came out while I was in high school, and through that I got into whole books by authors: *Howl*, of course, Denise Levertov's *The Jacob's Ladder*, Creeley's *For Love*, then later, O'Hara and Ashbery and Koch. There was so much going on in the Village at that time—a lot of music and poetry. I used to see Bob Dylan. I used to pass Gregory Corso on Sixth Avenue when I was only twelve. He was an idol in some sense. Like Rimbaud, he was the epitome of the "damned" poet, and so gorgeous!

At the same time that all this was whirling around me, I was carrying on my own adolescence filled with the usual traumas—boyfriends, girlfriends, other peoples' problems, parents, school. My own writing was based on my own experiences—the most weighty and juicy. The poems were perhaps influenced visually by e.e. Cummings. It was hard to identify with the so-called "academics," however. They really seemed stuck on the themes of aging and death. They'd been through the war—you know, *angst*, disillusionment. So I was going to work on my own "voice," as they say, inspired by what poetry as I experienced it can do—all those possibilities! And I guess I was attracted by the energy and outrageousness of the more off-beat writing. I also used to talk a lot in those days on the telephone and play the radio all night. Sometimes I think I've been more influenced by the telephone and radio that anything academic.

I went on to Bennington College, perhaps a little reluctantly, but it was supposed to be experimental. Well the school might have been, comparatively speaking, but the literature department was surprisingly stiff, although they had excellent professional novelists and poets as teachers who were very much involved with their own work. They set high standards and were living examples of real writers. The poet Howard Nemerov was a wonderful Blake and

Yeats teacher. You know Yeats' poem *The Cap and Bells?*
It's most strange and beautiful. The jester first sends his
soul dressed in blue to the young queen's casement and she
shuts her window. Then, he sends his heart in a red gar-
ment to her door and she waves it off with her fan. The
image of the disembodied soul and heart dressed in veils is
truly amazing. He dies, leaving the beloved his cap and bells
which finally possess her, and then the red one goes to her
right hand, and the blue to her left, whereupon they set up
a "noise like crickets."

College is a great place to lose yourself in reading. Nemerov's own poems exemplified a kind of irritation I could
only identify with abstractly at that point. However, Blake
seemed the complete opposite of an irritated projection on
the world. I would sit in on Francis Golffing's class on Rilke
simply to hear the German read outloud, though I couldn't
understand a word of it! Then, Bernard Malamud, the novelist, was encouraging in his attitude towards young writers.
He treated you as a potential writer rather than a dilettante.
Georges Guy, a Frenchman who had translated some Pierre
Reverdy poems with Kenneth Koch, gave a lot of personal
support as did Claude Fredericks, the exquisite printer. So,
the experience of being taken seriously in college was very
helpful, to say the least. At the same time, Ezra Pound
wasn't taught, nor Gertrude Stein, and I was finding John
Ashbery's *The Skaters,* when *Rivers & Mountains* came out,
more provocative than *The Wasteland.*

Ashbery's poem really is like a four-part symphony with
shifting voices and themes working through to some tenta-
tive acceptance of itself, nothing else. So that the poem is
the answer. He constantly plays with illusion and reality.
The image of skating brings with it the notion of parallel
lines that seem to meet when you look at them at a distance,
but of course never do. There's such subtlety and duplicity,
too, in Ashbery's poetry. It's great food for the head, and the
language is wonderfully surprising. "The day was gloves" is
one of my favorite lines. It says so much, but it's so silly too.
His goofy profundity seemed more interesting and far-out

than Eliot's. Eliot is great and useful, too, though he very likely did set things back, as Williams lamented. Anyway, I ended up doing my thesis on Theodore Roethke. The thesis was acceptable to Nemerov, but how much could you say after awhile about the theme of "journey"? Some of Roethke's poems are marvelous and escape—through their sheer music and childlike quality—being plodding, one-sided, completely dark. "I live between the heron and the wren./Beasts of the hill and serpents of the den." That's from *In a Dark Time.* I also included a sheaf of my own poems with the thesis.

By that time, however, (I graduated in 1966), I'd been out on my own and even started a poetry magazine, *Angel Hair,* with poet Lewis Warsh. We'd met at the Berkeley Poetry Conference, the summer of '65 at the Robert Duncan reading. The entire festival was a revelation, especially Charles Olson's notorious spontaneous rap and reading. I didn't stay for the whole thing, it was *too* painful. It was incredible to watch a poet seemingly enact his whole life—from infancy to old age—up there in front of you: very scary, but also moving, profound, and totally vulnerable. Up there without props, without a script, every idea of text or presentation tossed to the wind. Not giving you any sort of line, not dishing out some message or propaganda, whatever, but just opening up his head in public. Now this was an extreme occasion, but it's what I find most powerful about poetry readings, generally speaking. There's just someone up there doing his or her own music, relating to the audience's energy, and there's something very "on the line" and naked about the whole experience. Some of the best entertainers also get to this place at times, when something spontaneous happens and the room is elevated. With the best poets it's not rehearsed—that's not to say the words aren't there in front of them—it could be in the inflection, in the voice, in the body movement. So this all struck me full force at Berkeley, and I could really see the poet as a tribal shaman, speaking and moving and being embarassing not just for himself or herself, but for you, the audience.

Anyway, Berkeley '65 was an amazing series of events, much like the Kerouac Poetics situation here at Naropa, intense and exciting. I'd never heard so much poetry at one time and the scope was exceedingly broad—from Jack Spicer to Lenore Kandel to Dorn to Ginsberg to Berrigan. It also occurred to me that the contemporary poetry world was like a mandala—there was a poet for each psychological state or nuance—all these colors—and the poets complimented each other rather than being pitted against one another competitively. There was such variety and so much room—something for everyone, like the Bible, like Shakespeare. And there was room for younger poets and their visions.

For years before I moved there, the Lower East Side in New York City was a focal point for poets and poetic interchange in the form of numerous readings, magazines, publishing ventures, and stellar personalities. Diane di Prima's poetry newsletter *Floating Bear* flourished, as well as Ed Sanders' *Fuck You: A Magazine of the Arts*, and Ted Berrigan's *"C" A Magazine of the Arts*. By 1966, however, Diane was leaving the city and Ed's energies turned elsewhere. The readings at the Cafe Metro had moved to the Parish Hall at St. Mark's Church right across the street and during that year also, there was a grant from the Office of Economic Opportunity for a community arts project—theatre, film, and poetry, based at St. Mark's. I started working there right after college.

All this activity was blossoming ironically enough during the summer of Frank O'Hara's death—he had been such a catalyst between the uptown and downtown art worlds and suddenly a lot of energy was definitely downtown and on its own and involving many of the younger poets who had been acquainted with Frank. So there were readings and workshops and *The World* magazine, and endless gatherings and collaborations in poets' apartments. Much was learned and experienced by means of sheer determination, playfulness, and late-night hysteria. And then all your heroes would show up at the readings—Edwin Denby, Alex Katz, Andy

Warhol. My having an apartment nearby was a convenience
for everyone.

Ted Berrigan was a wonderful teacher for me at this
time, as he's been for many poets at some time or other. He
gave you instant honest feedback on your works and inspired you to write more. He showed us the value of working with—rather than against—surrounding verbal forms.
You know, for example, that Frank O'Hara could write with
a lot of things going on around him; he could write on the
telephone, on Fifth Avenue on his lunch hour, with the TV
on, people around, music. Some of his lines came from the
late show movies. He'd get up at a social gathering and go to
the typewriter and be able to toss something off, often bril-
liantly. And, knowing about this confidence of his—which
was shared by some of the younger writers, like Ted Berrigan and Ron Padgett—was assuring. Going on your confidence. Some kind of bully energy and trusting your own
mind and feeling your nimbleness and moving with speed
was tremendously inspiring.

Many surprising works were written in collaboration by a
shifting nexus of poets growing up together at that time. I'd
like to read a few works of mine from these years. This is
one called *Tape*:

O my life!

little political overcoats
                    ocean   human   hills   valleys
                                        & you breezy
la la la la la la la   Brooklyn
                            burglary & arson
        (fire   engine   siren   button   Nixon   puke)
Chicago
    over
San Diego
  OM AING GHRING CLING CHAMUNDA YEI VIJAY
                    blooming
into the light of Mike's eyes
                            very strange!

emerge

emerges
            such a sad light
                    weeps
                * * *
                Dope Fiends Unite
            & drive the vermin from our land
shou shou stereo
            it's Friday on this TV
        & the weak weather had star
                    Ted; howr y doin?
cloudy & cold
clear & mild
                            an energetic outlook
                            for an elephant
                * * *
Look out!
                It's the President's nose
            miles & miles of it
                    (snot)
                * * *
A mood sets in
            in Black hearts everywhere
                        it's a bad mood
                * * *
Repeating:
breathe in breathe out breathe in breathe out breathe in
breathe out
            now close your eyes
                    now open
                        now close
                            now open
now look inside!
                why it's me, see?
I'm a girl
            trapped in a mine
                    mine

OK. This is an open-ended input poem, with the radio on, obviously, and other persons present. I even spoke it into a tape recorder first—I wanted it to be that fast—and later transcribed it. But there's a concern with sound and what I chose to put in there. "Now look inside!" referred to opening the icebox. The repetition and play on the word "mine," after hearing about a mine disaster on the news, was very immediate. I have another later tape poem called *Baby Breakdown,* with an amusing history. While making this poem, I got a phone call from Ted Berringan, who was in London at the time, and it was incredibly garbled. I thought the Great Underground Cable was "freaking out," not a satellite, and so I go into a riff about that since all I could hear were parts of his words, fragments of his sentences. So it says in the poem:

PU AT IN ON YO EMS

(Translation: put that in one of your poems.)

Actually, this work was written at a very tragic point in my life, but you'd never know it—I could never write in or about those moods, really, though there must be some carry over. Bad moods never seemed a place for writing. I usually write out of some concentrated high energy place, though maybe that's changed a bit now. Also, in these works I'm talking to myself in a wacky way. And here's a "sestina," and what's a sestina? We'll check it out by reading one. Try Pound's *Sestina: Altaforte,* or John Ashbery's *Faust.* Here's mine, which is really about how to write one:

HOW THE SESTINA (YAWN) WORKS

I opened this poem with a yawn
thinking how tired I am of revolution
the way it's presented on television
isn't exactly poetry
You could use some more methedrine
if you ask me personally

People should be treated personally
there's another yawn
here's some more methedrine
Thanks! Now about this revolution
What do you think? What is poetry?
Is it like television?

Now I get up to turn off the television
Whew! It was getting to me personally
I think it is like poetry
Yawn it's 4 AM yawn   yawn
This new record is one big revolution
if you were listening you'd understand methedrine

isn't the greatest drug no not methedrine
it's no fun for watching television
You want to jump up have a revolution
about something that affects you personally
When you're busy and involved you never yawn
it's more like feeling, like energy, like poetry

I really like to write poetry
it's more fun than grass, acid, THC, methedrine
If I can't write I start to yawn
and it's time to sit back, watch television
see what's happening to me personally:
war, strike, starvation, revolution

This is a sample of my own revolution
taking the easy way out of poetry
I want it to hit you all personally
like a shot of extra-strong methedrine
so you'll become your own television
Become your own yawn!

O giant yawn, violent revolution
silent television, beautiful poetry
most deadly methedrine
                    I choose all of you for my poem personally

When I say in the sestina, "I choose all of you for my poem personally," I am talking about choosing the *words*. I'm choosing the words "methedrine," "revolution," "yawn"—not the ideas and experiences behind them, although they're there, of course. I'm not concerned with the experience of these words as ideas, or as influences behind the poem. These things—"acid," "THC"—are just entering the poem as words, really, that's how they're being used. I was writing poetry long before I took acid and long after. These words were on hand, right there, available. I'm just looking at them. You use what's right in front of you.

QUESTION: Did you start the poem with the words?

ANNE WALDMAN: Yes. I picked six words. That's usually how you begin a sestina. Or you might simply write a first verse of six lines and see what end words you come up with, see whether you can keep using them over again, through six verses and one final three-line verse. See if those words can be sustained. It's a real challenge to put them together in this combination. You should try to sustain a sestina sometime! I'd probably choose different words now, however: "ancipital," "marabout," "Carradine." I'm interested in words these days that I don't hear a lot in conversation.

Q: But everyone was into the expansiveness of the sixties in the same way.

A.W.: Yes, but individually, for their own expansion: this is *my* acid trip, I'm getting into *my* consciousness. In a way, all the mind travel separated people and now I think people are a little more generous about their expansion. Also not projecting your trips constantly onto situations. There's a little more space when you realize we're all kind of ordinary. Ordinary, with a little lime twist. What did you want to ask?

Q: I was just going to say that I felt after the sixties were over, looking back on them—for all the community feeling that happened, and there certainly was a lot—I felt there was meaningful communication . . .

A.W.: Down to earth communication.

Q: Because it was taken for granted.

A.W.: Yes, maybe. That's why poetry was always a salvation

in a way, because less was taken for granted. Or there was more happening, and also poetry's more timeless. You can't really pin it down to the sixties. I felt I had a lot of perspective simply through reading about the Surrealists, for example. There's a marvelous Dada anthology edited by Robert Motherwell, now out of print—but anyway, very exciting. Eric Satie's writing, Tristan Tzara's cut-ups, manifestos, and descriptions of early "theatre of the absurd" events, pictures of inanely constumed poets, etc. And this art was provoked by the politics and uptightness of the times. Or take Mayakovsky who, in 1912, in Russia, would show up at a public theatre wearing a top hat, a large wooden spoon in his lapel, reciting his poems through a megaphone. Artists have always been slightly "outside," or in advance of their time, and even now, we're still catching up to Gertrude Stein.

Q: This might not have anything to do with anything. You said a couple of minutes ago that you write when you're high and not when you're down . . .

A: Not necessarily high, but not horribly down, right. If I'm going through something very painful, where's the valium, you know?

Q: Yeah, yeah, but I find it interesting that during the sixties, during an incredibly depressed napalm period, there weren't many happy moments. And then as things are loosening up, you're moving into a space where you're exploring the darker side . . .

A.W.: I don't really polarize things into up or down. It's all everything—and you do make your own world. I think of the work from the sixties as energy pieces. I'm relating more to method than personal mood or content. The sheer energy or time it would take to accomplish a piece was interesting. I really felt the speed and heaviness of the sixties, and it was coursing through me. My attitude now has to do with growing up, perhaps. I'd never been through analysis or really used my dream-life to such an extent in my work. There's a female turf I'm exploring in *Journals & Dreams*, that I probably wouldn't have touched when I was twenty.

Something like that; you are where you are, you don't have to judge it, although some of the old poems might be more interesting than some I might write tomorrow.

Q: In *Baby Breakdown* I experienced the speediness of it, and it reveals a kind of pain. Now, it's like speeding past that . . .

Q: I don't think it's quite that—some kind of assertion of herself . . .

Q: Right. What I'm interested in is what was the impetus behind that?

A.W.: I was just going on my nerve. Dumb bully confidence. At school I was reading the classics, had a solid education, but if I let the masters take over—one would give up if you had to compare yourself with Yeats, Rilke, Shakespeare—especially a young student female poet! Where could I go? So I forgot a lot of what I learned and wrote very dumb, fast poems. Meeting cowboy poets—like Ed Sanders and Ted Berrigan and Dick Gallup, or reading Jack Kerouac and Allen Ginsberg and Diane di Prima—I mean, they weren't the epitome of WASP refinement or caution . . .

Q: That's what really surprised me, that you were able to come out of Bennington . . .

A.W.: Amnesia. After reading *Naked Lunch*, and John Ashbery, and having Frank O'Hara give you space, nothing was too crude or profane for poetry, which was fantastically exciting. No rules.

Q: What do you think now?

A.W.: Well, if everybody were writing the same way, it would be weird. You really have to figure it out for yourselves and trust your own heads. It would certainly be boring to be writing sixties poems—cosmic supermarket works.

Q: Does it strike you as sentimental now?

A.W.: No, but dated. When I read poems influenced by Allen's *America*, they're hard to relate to. Because it's already been done, and done appropriately. The ground's been covered. As far as influences go, someone like Philip Whalen or Lew Welch can give you a lot more space, for all time, in a sense.

Q: Well, how do you feel about coming down from that cosmic place?

A.W.: Well, I don't know how far I've been there, you know, personally in my work. The longer chants in *Fast Speaking Woman*, written more recently but earlier than *Journals & Dreams*, seem more cosmic than earlier work. And they were inspired by Allen Ginsberg and Kenneth Koch. Kenneth heard me read a piece called *100 Memories* and told me to continue to write long poems for awhile. He was excited about my vibrato, compared me to an opera singer. You know, just do it, write long and big. He writes enormous wonderful poems himself. And, of course, Allen Ginsberg's readings—his whole oral presentation was inspiring, and his personal encouragement was a real gift. I always had a self-conscious humorous way of commenting on what I was doing in the works—they couldn't just be completely one thing—purely political, for example. I think that's Kenneth's influence. Writing is too much fun.

Q: Is it really you in the poems? Not a persona?

A.W.: Well, I don't have one character going, if that's what you mean. . . .

Q: Could you say a little more about why you think Welch and Whalen give more space?

A.W.: Well, they're influenced by what they read, where they are, and the circuitries of their own thinking. And that input or whatever is available to you, as it is to them, although you might not write poems as good as theirs. Whereas Allen is all over the place, giving you the planet news, and it's hard to get up on the mountain like that all the time unless you're naturally there. You'd have to strain and that would make awful poetry. Philip puts you at ease in his works, though that's not to say the works are easy. He's brilliant and ordinary at the same time. Well, there are a lot of possible influences. I've spoken of Frank O'Hara. It's easier to sound like an O'Hara poem than really be one. It's tricky. Maybe these California poets give you more room than a poet living in New York City does. I have some poems written in Europe with O'Hara in mind, however. Just read a lot. Maybe you'll see what *not* to do.

I'd like to inject something about John Giorno here—my friendship with him and working with him. We worked together on the *Dial-A-Poem* record series and it was interesting to realize that he experienced poetry *completely* orally. All the editorial decisions were based on how the work sounded. He was much further into this than I was, and I think we influenced each other. When he was working with tapes, I got into tampering a bit with machines myself—different tracks and so forth, and he, in turn, started getting into solo raw performances. Before this, you never saw the poet John Giorno except at the control panel, and this was a part of the sixties too, perhaps—lights and multiple sound and acid punch at the door.

Q: Does Giorno write any poems anymore that aren't each line repeated?

A.W.: He's still working through that, extending that. Earlier poems in *The American Book of the Dead* don't repeat. Also, he uses "found objects" and poems on the page the way a visual artist might. I see him as coming through Duchamp's lineage. But on this record, he uses moogs, different tracks and it's really a sound piece. I'll play some cuts off these records later.

I'd like to move on a bit—we're moving fast and this is just a pittance of the whole picture, really, but I do want to read to you the "talking-to-the-sun" poems of Mayakovsky and O'Hara. If anything, these will give you a true sense of lineage, but also these are simply exceedingly beautiful poems and good to hear read aloud. These are "visitation" poems, and visionary and inspiring. OK, here's the Mayakovsky, I'll read a translation by Larry Fagin:

AN EXTRAORDINARY ADVENTURE
WHICH HAPPENED TO ME,
VLADIMIR MAYAKOVSKY,
IN A SUMMER COTTAGE

(Pushkino, Mount Akula, Rumyantsev Cottage,
   20 miles down the Yaroslav Railway)

140 suns blazed in one sunset,
rolling into July;
it was so hot
even the heat was sweating—
this was out in the country,
the village of Pushkino,
a little hump
at the foot of Mount Akula,
cracked roofs caving in.
Just outside of town
was a gaping hole,
and every evening
it slowly swallowed the sun.
In the morning
the sun would rise again
to flood the world
with yellow and red.
This happened
every day—
I was fed up with it.
One day I got so pissed off
everything turned white,
and I yelled at the sun:
"Get out of here,
you lazy bag of gas!
While you're loafing on a bed of clouds
I'm down here painting posters
all year 'round.
Look, Blondie,
how about showing a little humility;
come down to my place for a cup of tea!"
Uh-oh,
now I've done it!
Here he comes!
striding over the hill,

spreading his beaming steps
across the fields,
heading straight toward me!
I backed up slowly,
tried to show I wasn't afraid.
His eyes lit up the garden,
then his flaming head and shoulders
pressed against the windows,
doors,
and corners,
until he burst through
and spoke in a deep bass:
"Poet, for the very first time
I'm restraining myself,
so I won't burn you.
You called?
Well, pour the tea
and spread the jam!"
The heat was killing me—
my eyes filled with tears,
but I put the samovar on the fire
and said:
"Have a seat, comrade luminary!"
Some nerve I had,
shouting at him—
what had come over me?
I sat down,
completely confused,
not knowing what would happen next.
But a strange radiance
streamed from the sun,
and feeling more at ease,
I began to chat
about this
and that,
about how I'd been knocking myself out
doing publicity for ROSTA,
but the sun said:

"Okay,
calm down,
things aren't all that bad.
I suppose you think
it's easy for me
to shine;
you try it—
going around and around the world
shining your eyes out!"
We kept talking till it got dark,
till the night before, I mean.
How could there be darkness here?
We became pretty friendly
and soon
I was slapping him on the back
like he was a pal of mine,
and he said:
"You and I make quite a team,
old buddy!
Come on,
let's rise
and sing
and brighten up this drab world—
me with my sunshine,
you with your poems."
A wall of shadows,
a jail of nights
were shot down by our double-barreled suns.
And explosion of poetry and light—
shining in spite of everything!
And when the sun gets tired
at night,
I shine with all my might—
and day begins again,
shining everywhere,
forever shining,
till the end of time—
and to hell with everything else!

That's my motto—
and the sun's!

I'm sure the Mayakovsky is extraordinary in the original
Russian, especially read aloud. Russian poets are, for the
most part, tremendous orators, proclaiming their poems,
rolling their "r's," building to fantastic crescendos. You hear
this on recordings and in the live performances of
Yevtushenko and Voznesensky. Mayakovsky has been recorded, but not this particular poem to my knowledge. I assume some of you are familiar with Vladimir Mayakovsky?
No? Okay, he was born in 1893 in Bagdadi, Russia and died
on April 14, 1930, playing Russian roulette with himself.
He was a colorful and inventive Futurist. He was later the
official poet of the Russian Revolution, writing
propagandist works and painting posters. He visited Europe
and America in 1925. Later, he became disillusioned with
politics during the reign of Stalin and wrote a caustic, satirical play about the self-importance of party fat cats called
The Bedbug, which got him in a lot of trouble. He was always his own man, basically, and suffered the torments of
tempestuous love affairs and a high strung artistic tem-
perament. His poems have great humor and bite and energy. You should find out more about him and his work.
This particular poem was written in 1920.

"Rosta," by the way, is the abbreviation for the Russian
Telegraph Agency for which Mayakovsky and his group
produced thousands of hand-painted posters. I love the line,
"But a strange radiance / streamed from the sun," where
he's feeling the sun's love or vibration, not simply his heat.
Anthropomorphizing the sun is very funny, imagining his
shining eyes and his flaming head and shoulders. Might
make a great monster movie. The appellations are terrific—
"Blondie," "comrad luminary." The image of the sun
"loafing on a bed of clouds" is ironical. "uh-ho, / now I've
done it!" is wonderfully understated. It's such a good-
natured work.

Now, here's the O'Hara poem. Francis Russell O'Hara

was born June 27, 1926 in Baltimore, and died on July 25,
1966 after being struck by a beach buggy on the beach of
Fire Island. Very tragic, his death left a huge hole in the art
and poetry world. He was like the sun himself. And, like
Mayakovsky, a fantastic presence and energy in the work.
This poem is dated Fire Island, July 10, 1958:

A TRUE ACCOUNT OF TALKING
TO THE SUN AT FIRE ISLAND

The Sun woke me this morning loud
and clear, saying "Hey! I've been
trying to wake you up for fifteen
minutes. Don't be so rude, you are
only the second poet I've ever chosen
to speak to personally
                                so why
aren't you more attentive? If I could
burn you through the window I would
to wake you up. I can't hang around
here all day."
                        "Sorry, Sun, I stayed
up late last night talking to Hal."

"When I woke up Mayakovsky he was
a lot more prompt" the Sun said
petulantly. "Most people are up
already waiting to see if I'm going
to put in an appearance."
                                        I tried
to apologize "I missed you yesterday."
"That's better" he said. "I didn't
know you'd come out." You may be
wondering why I've come so close?"
"Yes" I said beginning to feel hot
wondering if maybe he wasn't burning me
anyway.
                "Frankly I wanted to tell you
I like your poetry. I see a lot

on my rounds and you're okay. You may
not be the greatest thing on earth, but
you're different. Now, I've heard some
say you're crazy, they being excessively
calm themselves to my mind, and other
crazy poets think that you're a boring
reactionary. Not me.
                    Just keep on
like I do and pay no attention. You'll
find that people always will complain
about the atmosphere, either too hot
or too cold, too bright or too dark, days
too short or too long,
                        If you don't appear
at all one day they think you're lazy
or dead. Just keep right on, I like it.

And don't worry about your lineage
poetic or natural. The Sun shines on
the jungle, you know, on the tundra
the sea, the ghetto. Wherever you were
I knew it and saw you moving. I was waiting
for you to get to work.
                        And now that you
are making your own days, so to speak,
even if no one reads you but me
you won't be depressed. Not
everyone can look up, even at me. It
hurts their eyes."
                    "Oh Sun, I'm so grateful to you!"

"Thanks and remember I'm watching. It's
easier for me to speak to you out
here. I don't have to slide down
between buildings to get your ear.
I know you love Manhattan, but
you ought to look up more often.
                                And
always embrace things, people earth

> sky stars, as I do, freely and with
> the appropriate sense of space. That
> is your inclination, known in the heavens
> and you should follow it to hell, if
> necessary, which I doubt.
>   Maybe we'll
> speak again in Africa, of which I too
> am specially fond. Go back to sleep now
> Frank, and I may leave a tiny poem
> in that brain of yours as my farewell."
>
> "Sun, don't go!" I was awake
> at last. "No, go I must, they're calling
> me."
>   "Who are they?"
>   "Rising" he said "Some
> day you'll know. They're calling to you
> too." Darkly he rose, and then I slept.

This poem strikes a deep chord for me. Mysterious and beautiful. Who, in fact, are "they"? Many times walking around New York City I hear an echo: "you ought to look up more often." It's a poem that becomes imprinted on you in a way. It's a great blessing.

I had too many ideas about poetry, which as I said, I forgot later. Nemerov liked one of my poems where, "I am a bird over the Harlem Valley at Wingdale," observing the inmates of a nuthouse. Actually, I had a dear friend in the madhouse. The obvious point was, I can fly, and I'm locked up. But there was a list in there: "I have seen this and I have seen that," which really worked. His encouragement helped. Half the battle is just having someone say, like the Sun, "Just keep right on, I like it." And then the more you do the more you get in touch with what you're doing.

Q: How did the change happen in you?

A.W.: It happened gradually. I felt I was evolving with a whole community of younger writers as well, connecting with Michael Brownstein's work, Bernadette Mayer's, and so on. I loosened up. I realized that poetry didn't have to be a

private or a classroom affair. We all gave each other feedback. And we worked together on magazines, and wrote collaborations.

Q: Was *Fast Speaking Woman* written when you were off
by yourself?

A.W.: *Fast Speaking Woman* is still going on, it's intermi-
nable. It began as a journal work, a list, fill in the blanks
around the word "woman" piece, but constantly playing
with the sound of other words in my head. It began in South
America and later Michael Brownstein gave me a copy of
the Maria Sabina recording, which was completely relevant.
The piece is a re-working of how this Mazatec Shamaness
handles language. I feel close to shaman energy, but anyway,
I was writing this poem on airplanes, in hotels, at home, and
so on.

Q: Things just popped into your head?

A.W.: Often, but sometimes they're triggered by what you
see outside your head. In the poem *Light & Shadow* there's a
list of great men who contributed something to humankind.
I was sitting at a poetry reading in Oregon, surrounded by
classical sculptored heads and busts of all these guys and
jotted their names down and started embellishing on what
they conjured up for me in terms of light and shadow: "Socrates' wise forehead, Einstein's brain the speed/of light . . . ,"
and so on.

Q: I thought it was visual rather than intellectual.

A.W.: Partially—light and shadow *are* visual, of course. But
in this section, it was fast hits on all the characters in the au-
ditorium. There's Goethe's bust, and I know Goethe's book
Elective Affinities, and it's one of my favorite books, so I just
put in "Goethe's elective affinities." Herodotus was up there,
and I'd read and adored his book the *Histories*, so I wrote,
"Herodotus collecting light: knowledge of/cats, Egypt's
black ways & foreign women." "Dante spiralling upward to
stars" is right out of the *Commedia*. "Darwin, Rousseau,
Descartes all thinking/in their armchairs" is one of my favorite lines. It was a funny visual image. So, this part of the
poem was playfully arrived at, you know? Not a serious

meditation on the heavyweights. Then, I went on adding more names. I'd recently seen Cecil Taylor playing in San Francisco and he was literally spinning webs of light with his hands, but "wave breaking fingers/on the black & white keys" seemed more accurate. The work went through several arrangements with different parts inserted.

Q: What about your work *Paul Eluard*?

A.W.: That's a little portrait of the man, but I also consider him an influence. His poems are marvelously simple and he's good-hearted. I have an early poem that ends "When I close my eyes, I kill you world," which was influenced by him. Sei Shonagon's *Pillow Book*, written at the time of the Heian Court in tenth-century Japan, was also an influence around the same time. Her lists are terrific, very humorous.

Q: You said something about using *La Vita Nuova* last Year?

A.W.: Well, I've written a little suite of love poems, about ten pages, using real life, cut-up method, fiction, and I'm working on a text explaining how the poems were arrived at, the way Dante does in *La Vita Nuova*. Dante's a great source. I have a poem entitled *My Lady*, definitely inspired by the poems in Dante's book.

Q: What kind of voice were you using? Who was the lady and who was the person writing about the lady?

A.W.: I think I was in an elevated place, like the troubadour poets. I felt myself in the eleventh century and inspired by the idea of the Lady Liege, who's not your wife or true companion, but the unattainable ideal. The Muse. Yet, I also had a particular woman in mind.

Q: Do you ever try to write a poem in a voice that isn't directly your own experience, like a man's or someone else's?

A.W.: Well, I move in and out of being George Sand in a portrait entitled *George Sand*. Know who she was? Not exactly a man. A female novelist who smoked big cigars. Author of *Indiana, Lavinia, The Haunted Pool*, and many other books. Very prolific. So, I just wrote a meditation—I'd been reading about her life, sometimes becoming her, identifying with her energy. There's a companion piece to this entitled *Balzac*, and that has something to do with using nineteenth-century language. I love novels, and what characters say in them. Inveterate romantic, I guess.

But generally, I get more interested in longer pieces, in sustaining a musical theme, rather than worrying about one voice. I think more about the configurations of the words "light" and "shadow." Light and shadow are no longer simply subject matter after you say them fifty times, right? It moves around. It's musical. Read *Lifting Belly* by Gertrude Stein. Here, she repeats and varies the phrase "lifting belly" until it becomes like breathing.

Q: Jackson Mac Low uses repetitions too.

A.W.: Yes, he repeats words and works with sound variations. His pieces are sound meditations. But you know, there is some aesthetic choice involved with the words you want to repeat. If I kept repeating the word "cockroach," I'd make myself sick, I think . . .

Q: As opposed to describing all the cockroach's activities, which you consider an academic procedure . . .

A.W.: Well, it depends on how it's done. Neruda could do it great!

Q: Would you say that words are like notes or are they chords?

A.W.: Well, actually, both. Let's see if I can make you hear this: "I'm the gadget woman, I'm the druid woman, I'm the evil woman." Listen I'm going to move things around: "I'm the Ebo woman, I'm the Yoruba woman, I'm the vibrato woman. I'm the woman with the keys, I'm the woman with the glue." I can hear the changes and the difference between the notes and the chords, but I can't name what I'm doing.

Q: It's like heart beats. With different emotions the heart beat will speed up or slow down.

A.W.: Right. Something like that.

Q: Two big themes: analysis and Buddhism. How do you feel those two things have worked into your work? I mean, the work as talking to yourself and as self-revelation. And work on neurosis.

A.W.: Well, as I said before, I've never been in analysis.
But I felt that much of the work in *Journals & Dreams* was
as if I might be, because it's using as source material a lot of
stuff dredged-up from the so-called "unconscious"—fantasies,
dreams. It has a confessional quality, it goes below the surface a lot more, although I still consider the writing playful,
experimental, and involving sound. Some of the pieces seem
strictly for the page, not to be read aloud, too private or
something. As for Buddhism, the connection goes way back.
There's always been some attraction—it's a psychological
practice that makes sense to me. You're prostrating to your
own mind, trusting that. There's no god involved. It's about
becoming a warrior, making yourself impeccable. So, it runs
parallel to art in some way in that you're working on a refining process. And it's a process. It involves a discipline,
like writing and constant work with your own ego. But I
can't stand jargon or concept words in poetry, and so the
Buddhist lingo doesn't enter my works, although the Bud-
dha is welcome anytime. Maybe I've gotten slightly
perfectionistic about my work, a little harder on myself. Edwin Denby, the poet and dance critic, has always been my
root-guru, and he has no particular connection to the Buddhist system, per se. But the practice helps you work on
your sanity, helps you see what's right in front of you, cuts
through a lot of unnecessary static. I'm also interested in
some of my pieces coming out of psychological states that I
can get detached from, or can look at. One piece of writing
is all red, for example, and seems to have something to do
with anger and aggression, though none of those things—not
even the color red—is ever mentioned. Another piece, *Divorce Work* is a collage, trying to make some order out of actual events, dreams, fantasies, Spanish words, the reality of
the harshness of the Lower East Side, using Dante's
Purgatorio as an inspiration and source.

OK, we're running short. I'd like to close by playing some
things to you off the Giorno Poetry Systems anthologies that
might inspire you further. First, I'd like to play a Charles
Olson cut, *The Ridge*. He's sick here, his lungs laboring,

you can hear the breathing. There's an eerie wind blowing through this piece. [*Plays.*] And lastly, Frank O'Hara's *Ode to Joy.* "No more dying," folks. [*Plays.*]

ODE TO JOY

We shall have everything we want and there'll be no more dying
  on the pretty plains or in the supper clubs
for our symbol we'll acknowledge vulgar materialistic laughter
  over an insatiable sexual appetite
and the streets will be filled with racing forms
and the photographs of murderers and narcissists and movie stars
  will swell from the walls and books alive in steaming rooms
  to press against our burning flesh not once but interminably
as water flows down hill into the full-lipped basin
and the adder dives for the ultimate ostrich egg
and the feather cushion preens beneath a reclining monolith
  that's sweating with post-exertion visibility and sweetness
  near the grave of love

                             No more dying

We shall see the grave of love as a lovely sight and temporary
  near the elm that spells the lovers' names in roots
and there'll be no more music but the ears in lips and no more wit
  but tongues in ears and no more drums but ears to thighs
as evening signals nudities unknown to ancestors' imaginations
and the imagination itself will stagger like a tired paramour of ivory
  under the sculptural necessities of lust that never falters
  like a six-mile runner from Sweden or Liberia covered with gold
as lava flows up and over the far-down somnolent city's abdication
and the hermit always wanting to be lone is lone at last
and the weight of external heat crushes the heat-hating Puritan
  who's self-defeating vice becomes a proper sepulchre at last
  that love may live

Buildings will go up into the dizzy air as love itself goes in
  and up the reeling life that it has chosen for once or all
while in the sky a feeling of intemperate fondness will excite the birds
  to swoop and veer like flies crawling across absorbed limbs
that weep a pearly perspiration on the sheets of brief attention
and the hairs dry out that summon anxious declaration of the organs
  as they rise like buildings to the needs of temporary neighbors
  pouring hunger through the heart to feed desire in intravenous ways

like the ways of gods with humans in the innocent combination of light
and flesh or as the legends ride their heroes through the dark to found
great cities where all life is possible to maintain as long as time
   which wants us to remain for cocktails in a bar and after dinner
   lets us live with it

No more dying

Selected Sources

ALLEN, DONALD, *The New American Poetry, 1945-60* (New York: Grove Press, 1960).

ASHBERY, JOHN, "Faust," *The Tennis Court Oath* (Wesleyan University Press, 1962), pp. 47-48.

————, "The Skaters," *Rivers & Mountains* (New York: Holt, Rinehart & Winston, 1966).

BURROUGHS, WILLIAM, *Naked Lunch* (New York: Grove Press, 1959).

CREELEY, ROBERT, "For Love," from *Selected Poems* (New York: Scribner's Sons, 1962), pp. 1-37.

DENBY, EDWIN, *Collected Poems* (New York: Full Court Press, 1976).

ELIOT, T.S., *The Wasteland* (New York: Harcourt, Brace & World, Inc., 1934).

GINSBERG, ALLEN, *Howl* (San Francisco: City Lights Books, 1976).

GIORNO, JOHN, *Dial-A-Poem* Record Series (New York: Giorno Poetry Systems).

————, *The American Book of the Dead* (Berkeley: Bookpeople, Mother Press, 1967).

LEVERTOV, DENISE, *The Jacob's Ladder* (New York: New Directions Publishing, 1961).

MAYAKOVSKY, VLADIMIR, "An Extraordinary Adventure That Happened to Me, Vladimir Mayakovsky, in a Summer Cottage," trans. Larry Fagin. Used by permission of the translator. Copyright ©1976 Larry Fagin. Thanks to Bill Berkson's *Big Sky* Magazine.

MAYER, BERNADETTE, "Studying Hunger (Big Sky/Adventures in Poetry)," *Memory* (Plainfield, Vt.: North Atlantic Books).

MORRIS, IVAN, trans., *The Pillow Book of Sei Shonagon* (New York: Columbia University Press, 1967).

MOTHERWELL, ROBERT, ed., *The Dada Painters and Poets* (New York: Wittenborn, Schultz, Inc., 1951).

O'HARA, FRANK, "Ode to Joy," from the *Dial-A-Poets 1972* (Recorded in New York, 1963). Version of the poem in *The Collected Poems of Frank O'Hara,* ed. Don Allen (New York: Alfred A. Knopf, Inc., 1972), p. 281. Reprinted by permission of the publisher.

———, "A True Account of Talking to the Sun at Fire Island," op. cit. Reprinted by permission of the publisher.

OLSON, CHARLES, "The Ridge," *Disconnected, Dial-A-Poem II* Record Series (New York: recorded at S.U.N.Y. at Cortland, October 20, 1967).

POUND, EZRA, "The River Merchant's Wife: A Letter," *Selected Poems of Ezra Pound* (New York: New Directions, 1957), p. 52.

———, "Sestina: Altaforte," op. cit., p. 7.

REYNOLDS, BARBARA, trans., Dante's *La Vita Nuova* (New York: Penguin Books, 1969).

ROETHKE, THEODORE, "In a Dark Time," *The Far Field* (New York: Doubleday, Anchor Books, 1971), p. 79.

SABINA, MARIA, "Mushroom Ceremony of the Mazatec Indians of Mexico," recorded by Z.P. and R.G. Wasson (Folkways, 1966).

WALDMAN, ANNE, "Baby Breakdown," *Baby Breakdown* (Indianapolis, Ind.: Bobbs-Merrill Co., 1970).

———, "Balzac," *Journals & Dreams* (New York: Stonehill Publishing, 1976), p. 68.

———, "Divorce Work," op. cit., pp. 113-115.

———, *Fast Speaking Woman* (San Francisco, City Lights Books, Pocket Poets No. 33, 1975).

———, "George Sand," *Journals & Dreams,* op. cit., p. 67.

———, "How the Sestina (Yawn) Works," *Baby Breakdown,* op. cit., p. 15. Reprinted by permission of the author.

———, "I'm the gadget woman," *Fast Speaking Woman,* op. cit.

———, "Light & Shadow," op. cit.

———, "My Lady," *Journals & Dreams,* op. cit.

———, *O My Life!* (New York: Angel Hair Books, 1968).

_____, "100 Memories," *No Hassles* (New York: Kulchur Foundation, 1971).

_____, "Paul Eluard," *Baby Breakdown*, op. cit., p. 32.

_____, "Tape," *Baby Breakdown*, op. cit., pp. 20-21. Reprinted by permission of the author.

Photo by Andrea Craig

Miguel Algarin

VOLUME AND VALUE OF THE BREATH IN POETRY

AUGUST 3, 1976

I

VOLUME AND VALUE OF THE BREATH
IN POETRY READINGS OUTDOORS

THERE ARE THREE points I want to talk about. The first one is about volume and value of the breath in poetry readings outdoors. The second is about volume and value of the breath indoors: The Nuyorican Poets' Cafe. The third point is about reading versus hearing.

About five days before I came to Naropa Institute I was invited to do a poetry reading at Central Park, Sheep's Meadow. It was a salsa band concert—you know what salsa is? It's New York Puerto Rican, very fast, rhythmic, percussive popular music. I thought there were going to be about 1000 or 2000 people, so I figured that would probably be the biggest audience I had ever faced. When I got there, there were 28,000 people and one of the best salsa bands in the city had played right before me. The band left people screaming and shouting and all worked up. Then, "Now Miguel Algarin is going to read," and 28,000 people went BOOOOO. I walked up to the mike and looked out. I really felt nervous and tense, so I took a deep breath and let out

325

the loudest, strongest, and most sustained sound I could get out of me. As I did that, the crowd began to shut up, and the boos stopped. Right at the highest pitch and loudness that I could go to, over the enormous speakers that they had, I started the poem. I slipped into their consciousness. They had been made into one by the salsa band immediately before me. But the emcee, instead of just letting me slip into a poem, had to announce that poetry was going to be done, and that had broken the sound thread.

My first point is about volume, value, and breath outdoors. It seems that it's popular for poets to read their work as if they were not permitted to help the poem along. They read their work in the palest, least inflected, softest, most boring tones. Why that should be, I don't know. But that is what I find happening everywhere. This isn't a problem for street poets. When a New York street poet recites on Sixth Street and Avenue A, he cannot afford to sound pale and unengaging, because the principles are different. People are on the move. There is no tradition of people on the sidewalk handing over their attention. The poet has to get out there and project a volume that stops the crowd and concentrates it into a listening body. The success with which a poet can do this determines his reputation in the community, as poet.

Miguel Piñero and Lucky CienFuegos are veteran poets of street readings. When we started to do streetcorner readings we were all having the same problem. We had to find a way to stop the crowd and turn it into ears instead of tongues. Lucky CienFuegos taught me a lot on this point. Lucky always starts his street readings with a poem to Lolita Lebron. She is a Puerto Rican Nationalist who shot at members of the U.S. Congress in 1954. She was put into jail and is still there. Her motives are very real. People are passing, talking, a lot of beer is being drunk, a lot of pot is being smoked, and everybody's broke. Lucky begins:

FREEEEEE THAT SISTER
FREE THAT LOVING LOVING

LOOOOOVING SISTER
FREE THAT WOMAN FREE THAT LOVING
LOVING WOMAN
FREE LOLITA LEBRON

Sister Sister don't you know a Brother
is not always a Brother
A Brother seems to say Peace and
Power. Peace and Power.
A Sinner is not always a Sinner
but how could you communicate it
to them,
who understand only hate.
Life seems to say to Lolita Lebron
Love is stronger than thunder
but Death keeps kissing both of
her cheeks.
In the magnifying glass of the Revolutionary's eyes
they see the Fox tricked by the
Lions,
and Justice Justice Justice
they seem to call it
but how ugly how dry
is the word Justice
They seem to say
Just us, Just them
I seem to call
Capitalistic Swine.

Lucky reaches his loudest volume, you are bound to get a street crowd. You've done another thing with that volume too. You've caused a crowd to start responding. Open uncontrolled sound makes people respond. They not only give you their attention, but they're also at that point where attention is not passive but active. Your poetry goes into a crowd that is going to read you back the moment that the poetry gets boring or falls off.

Big open uncontrolled sound is not the only possibility for street poetry, but it's the primary way to stop a crowd. Once you've stopped them and you keep them at that passive-listening but willing-to-react stage, you can create almost anything on a street corner, primarily theater. Volume should be used as an active force. Everybody that reads poetry should discover the range of the voice.

The next problem that the poet faces is talking about his pain in a way that leaves him free to talk about a solution to that pain. He does this through the poem by examining himself in front of people so that they can get into the habit of doing it for themselves. There is no meditation, and there are no sittings for factory laborers.

The way that the poet makes himself responsible for teaching the people how to think about themselves, and how to put time out for thinking about themselves, is for him to do it, and do it aloud, and do it where people will hear him. It's a responsibility that all poets have. Miguel Piñero, Lucky, and myself have taken it on. We read our poetry not only on street corners, but in apartments, so that people can get to hear us examining ourselves. In the process you discover that poets are of all ages. The youngest poet in the Nuyorican Poetry Anthology is nine years old. But first I'm going to read you a poem by Martita Morales. It's an interesting poem because Martita was feeling a great deal of pain and she was exploring it. Her pain had to do with a racial situation, which wasn't about black against white, but about her family against her boyfriend. The boyfriend had an afro and his hair was a throwback to blackness, instead of a "forward" step toward straight hair:

THE SOUNDS OF SIXTH STREET

Kids with innocent minds
and their curiosity aroused

"¿Mami, porque tu blanca y papi tan?"

your curiosity aroused you into asking the question
your curiosity was wandering
you wondered why all the spanish speaking people
are of many different colors

"Chocolate
hey nene
mira
Chocolate
hey mira
ven aca Chocolate"

but he kept on running
and
you had no knowledge
that
that wasn't his name
but the name of his color
which was Tan or Brown
you did not know
that
the Puerto Rican people
are a mixture of
many different races
you do not know
for you are
so young
and so innocent
and when your mother
would take you to the park
or in the summer
to the beach
where you play in the sand
with many different people
people—
men and women of your age
that range from about 3-5
you do not know
for they are all
beautiful people
because you can all play
get along
and be in a world of your own

but as the child gets older
she rebels
rebels against the fact
that
her parents will not let her have a boyfriend
with an afro
or con el pelo grifo
because he looks black
and black to them is dirty
but dead and silky blond hair
with blue eyes
and white skin
is supposed to be pure

I'll stop the poem there because what happens to Martita is that she realizes her mother is teaching her to make racial distinctions.

BOBBIE LOUISE HAWKINS: So she's actually talking about black and black.

MIGUEL ALGARIN: Right, that's very accurate. The mother, in fact, is making the racist discrimination between black and black, what's blacker is worse. But Martita catches on and can analyze that in her parents. Unfortunately, the analysis falls off there, doesn't go all the way, and she's left hating the whites, although, as you caught on, in the earlier part of the poem, she says that when men and women are ages three and five, they can get along and create a society of their own. As the years go on, however, all of the imposition from the parent starts to come in. Martita picks up the racist attitudes of the parents against the blackness that they themselves have. It's at that point that the poem shifts. She gets lost into an inverted racism where she talks against the white man as the devil. When Martita does this poem on the street, she gets into a conversational tone for a while, and then she yells, "Chocolate, Hey, Mira, Chocolate." It is an attention grabber, her manipulation of the volume of her voice. She grabs the crowd, and then goes back into her story-telling.

Next, I'll read "The Book of Genesis according to St. Miguelito." This is another level of poetry on the streets as we are working it. The first one was Lucky's technique. He has a huge voice. He's a little guy, about five feet, four inches, with an afro that goes out, totally electric. Then his mouth opens and this huge sound comes out. Martita does something else. She gets into a little conversational piece, and all of the sudden she opens up her volume and then she comes back and talks.

Miguel Piñero spent a lot of time in jail, so his rap and consciousness of poetry is heavily influenced by the oral jailhouse tradition. What you get with Miguel is a consciousness of black rhythms. This poem is known as the Bible of the Slums. It's a great mythological poem in that he completely reverses the explanation of the divine person. The people get into that, they love it. They check out what they've been fed and what Miky's doing. That gives them a distance, a point of reference, a perspective to look at the self, and that's the object:

THE BOOK OF GENESIS ACCORDING TO SAINT MIGUELITO

> Before the beginning
> God created God
> In the beginning
> God created the ghettos & slums
> and God saw this was good.
> So God said,
> "Let there be more ghettos & slums"
> and there were more ghettos & slums.
> But God saw this was plain
> so
> to decorate it
> God created leadbase paint
> and then
> God commanded the rivers of garbage & filth
> to flow gracefully through the ghettos.
> On the third day
> because on the second day God was out of town

On the third day
God's nose was running
& his jones was coming down and God
in his all knowing wisdom
he knew he was sick
he needed a fix
so God
created the backyards of the ghettos
& the alleys of the slums
& heroin & cocaine
and
with his divine wisdom & grace
God created hepatitis
who begat lockjaw
who begat malaria
who begat degradation
who begat
GENOCIDE
and God knew this was good
in fact God knew things couldn't git better
but he decided to try anyway
On the fourth day . . .

Now if I had been doing this right, the value of the
breath is the length or the period of time that you can hold
it, and keep it going, so that your reading is not choppy.
You're not reading one line, and another line, line (breath)
line (breath) line (breath), which is very boring. The
pressures of reading on the street are so strong that once you
catch a breath, and you got a line going out of yourself, you
try to keep that line really moving. Your object is not to in-
terrupt yourself with constant short breaths, but to bring it
in and start it out. You keep it going until you've created a
sentence that is total and complete. All eyes are on you and
your eyes are on them, then, you breathe again. It's very important, because you're like an instrument, and an instrument has disciplines. We feel this discipline because it's so
hard to keep attention. There is a very generous situation in

this classroom, where everybody is willing to give me their attention. Usually it's the other way around. You try to grasp that attention, hold it, and put it on yourself until you show something about yourself that someone else needs to see.

I'm going to read to you Georgie Lopez. He's the youngest poet, he's nine years old. I'll tell you how he writes his poems. Georgie comes into the house and dictates the poem to anyone in the house who can type. He can't write or read, which is a problem because New York schools are not vehicles for learning how to read and write. So we were content that he did dictate the poems, but it wasn't enough. He had to do something else. He had to indicate to us where the line stopped. Otherwise whoever typed would sit there and invent the lines for him. He'd just do a little rap which would be taken down, but then he wouldn't know anything about a line and the value of a line. So we got into the habit of typing it as he said it, and then demanding from him that whenever he was finished with a thought, he had to let us know:

ABOUT THE RATS

The rats sell drugs
they take it—they use it—
they stick themselves with dirty
needles
They use it in the Bronx
they get into cocaine like they get into
the billiard clubs
they play nodding out pool
they are behind the eight ball
georgie lopez will be the DDT against
the rats
they get into the basements
with a gang of grass and coke
The rats sell to old men
old ladies and to young people like
me georgie lopez

But georgie lopez is the DDT against
the rats
I am the rat poison that will get into
the corner of the corner of the streets
oh man, yeah, man yes there are plenty of
rats and we need more cats
the cats will have a war against the
rats very soon
I know, I know, because I am
georgie lopez DDT against the
Rats.

What I found very valuable about what he was writing
was that it clued me to where he saw his enemies, what
caused his fear. This is a description of his world. The rats
are both themselves and a symbol for the dope addicts that
made Georgie's life really miserable. His mother can't hold
on to a radio or a T.V., it just disappears. It worried mē
when this nine-year-old boy showed his inner world and his
inner world was a vision of himself as DDT. He's a hero,
but I would have preferred for Georgie to open himself up
to find a healthy planet.

A kid on the street is not cute like you would think. You
put a kid on a street corner to recite a poem, and you think
people would stop and say, "look how cute." Well it doesn't
happen. They pass him right by. We're trying to get him to
understand volume, value, and the breath, and how to control it, and from there how to manipulate the crowd so that
they stand there and listen. Once, we got him to the point of
reciting his own poems, the power of his words was great. At
those moments words are medicinal. Georgie Lopez stands
there talking about Me, Georgie Lopez, I'm the DDT that's
cutting through everybody's consciousness. He is nine, he
looks nine, he's a fat tough little kid. His words come into
the body and they change your chemistry right on the spot.
People do not go away to analyze Georgie's poem. They will
have understood and have experienced what happened right

there. The registering will have been performed. The change will have been performed too.

II

VOLUME AND VALUE:
THE NUYORICAN POETS' CAFE

Now I want to talk about the Nuyorican Poets' Cafe, which is my second point. So far we've been talking about poetry outdoors, but now we will talk about poetry indoors and the economy of that move. We realized that we were being summer poets and nothing else because we had not worked the streetcorners in winter. Only the Salvation Army does that.

Miky, Lucky, and I started to read around town, but we found that there was a problem with that. The poetry circuit in New York is a very closed circuit. It's hard to pry it open, and when you do, it has few surprises. The people who are there are already in the groove of things. They're looking for poetry, they come to hear poetry. You're not really adding folks to the roster, you're just performing for those who want to hear it. It's not bad, but it's not rewarding to us. All of the poetry programs that exist in New York are usually outside of communities like the Lower East Side. Most often the place is a West Village Bar, or a library, and that's not where the people we wanted to read to come. They will not come. Even though we are becoming popular among college students, so that Puerto Rican college students will come to a reading, say, at St. Marks Church, we can't get our neighborhood people from Avenue A and Sixth Street to come to Second Avenue and Tenth Street to hear poetry. We had to take it indoors, and I had to find a way to do it. So I opened a cafe.

Now the cafe is a very special place for me, because I never thought that I would own a cafe, and I definitely never thought that I would sell wine and beer to anybody. So when I opened it up, I tried selling coffee and fruit juices and lost the audience. Then I put in beer and wine, no hard liquor, and people bought it.

Miguel Piñero had become really famous by the time I decided to open the cafe. He had written a play *Short Eyes* that won the New York Drama Critics Award, the Obie Award, and got nominated for the Tony Awards. Then all of the New York cultural chic started to come around us, and they are like vultures. Miky had the story of the century, ex-convict come out of jail, writing an award-winning play. The media had made a discovery. The press, everybody, everybody wanted to feed off that image. So when I first opened the cafe, I was afraid that the poetry circuit people would come but not the neighborhood people. I tried to find a way to break that.

I did it without knowing, and I'll tell you how I did it. We sat down and had a meeting, the three of us, Miky, Lucky, and I. We talked about what we were going to do and what prices to charge. Miky and Lucky said, "we should get $1.25 a drink," and I said, "I can't even afford that, can you?" We admitted we couldn't. Then Miky went off on tour, and Lucky was off into his private world. That caused a split between us. I didn't agree to their prices. So what happened was that it was left up to me. I put the price at 50¢ on the wine and the beer. It was the cheapest price around town, and we served a whole mug of beer too.

I didn't know what that economic move had done. I didn't really understand that until later. It meant that at 50¢ we would get street people, and at 50¢ we would have automatically knocked out the chic. Why? Because a place where a drink is sold for 50¢ is suspect, and the people who buy drinks at 50¢ are dangerous. I found, for example, that Puerto Rican lawyers, judges, and doctors won't come. They're afraid. Only politicians like Herman Badillo come, because he's hoping for votes.

So what happened in that situation was that I had done something that was very valuable without being aware of it. I had made my place a home for oral poetry. All of a sudden, folks like Ginsberg, Burroughs, Ferlinghetti came to

the cafe to read. On any given night, any young poet in the
city could come to read. I'd put him up but he'd take his
risk. The risks are that if the crowd is itchy and they are
bored by you, they'll confront you.

Jack Brown once came down and was reading very soft
love poetry. Cuca who was drunk by that time said, "What's
that shit about?" Jack said, "It's just a love poem to women."
She said, "A man can't write a love poem to women." And
she said, "Only women know how to love women. You see
this kid, you see this belly." (She was pregnant.) "Some
cocksucker did that to me and he's not writing me any love
poems." Jack didn't know what to do, so he sat down. But
the thing to do is to continue reading. Just center yourself
in yourself. If Cuca really gets out of hand, what I do is to
stop the poet. Then I just turn the thing over to Cuca. I
said, "O.K. Jack, wait, wait. Cuca go ahead, take the stage."
I'll tell you the story of what happened that night. She did
take it, and she frightened me because she was pregnant and
very drunk. She started to dance, and was spinning around
the room with this huge belly on her, and she was drunk. I
thought she was going to fall, so all of us were chasing after
her, letting her do her dance so that she'd shut up and sit
down. You can't put a woman like Cuca out. She's a great
poet, and a great dancer. She was really angry at her man,
and was getting drunk over it, and we couldn't put her out.
I turned the stage over to her, and she decided she was going to do this wild dance, nine months pregnant. All we
could do was move around and try to catch her if she fell—
we had to deal with it.

But I was into the economy of poetry. The place had become a cultural center where poets and writers could come
to read and hang out for hours. It was very important, that
50¢. I haven't paid rent for a year though.

As a matter of fact, I had the city marshals at the door a
day before I left for here. A very beautiful thing happened.
He came with his padlocks, and with these huge clippers.
They can clip any lock you got on your door. They were
coming to close the cafe down. I didn't say anything to any-

body, because I wanted to avoid as much as possible any confrontation. Confrontation could wind me up in jail, beaten up by the cops and a lot of people sympathizing with me. But I'm not a martyr that way.

So I tried to keep it quiet, but then when the marshal arrived he was stunned. He came with his sirens blaring, mucho gold star badge, a gun, and his clippers. Well, within seconds, all the people who loved the cafe, who come there every Thursday through Sunday, were gathering in front of the place. I hadn't talked to anybody. I didn't want any fuss. I knew that someone, a friend of mine from the community, would ultimately confront the marshal. The marshal would probably start something with him, and I'd be in the middle. I'd be the one that gets carted away. I hadn't told anybody that the marshal was coming. But they all started to gather, and I gave them the cold shoulder. The marshal didn't understand my logic. He said, "I'm gonna close up the place," and made a move to clip the lock. The whole crowd bristled, and this man realized that he was in for a bad whipping. He put his clippers away, got in his car, and went away. Now some of these guys, by the way, are very rich. These marshals don't just get paid by the city. They get a percentage on every closure. They also have the power of entrance, entering your space, so they can walk out, and do walk out with the most valuable property in their pockets. Some of these marshals make as much as $100,000 a year. But he didn't make any off us.

The cafe then took poetry indoors where the vocal problems were different. It wasn't about screaming out as loud as you could to rivet attention on yourself. It was about controlling volume to make it as interesting as the street corner reading. You can't just scream at people in close quarters and expect them to feel good about it. Even when they agree with your perspective and your rap, they don't want to be screamed at. So the poets became very sophisticated about tonal variations. They started to control volume, but not lose those varieties in vocal projection that makes things exciting to listen to. What this also did was to add a subtlety to the poetry, in its content. I believe volume is deeply connected to content. When you have to trim the volume of the breath to the size of the room you're in, it does something to the content of the poetry. The poetry became subtler, it had other dimensions, it became much more personal, though it still retained the great vocal variety that I say is important in reading. There are questions so I'm going to stop for a moment.

QUESTION: That poem you read by Miguel Piñero reminded me very much of the sort of political things that Lawrence Ferlinghetti was writing in the 50's, and I wonder if there is any connection there?

M.A.: Prior to Ferlinghetti being at the cafe and Miky meeting Ferlinghetti there, I don't think they knew each other.

Q: I think in the first poem you mentioned the word, is it *Vaya,* twice—is that a sound or is that a word with a meaning?

M.A.: It's an expletive, it means Right ON! Get it! Real! Vaya! That's what it means.

Q: The kind of poetry that you're talking about seems to have two qualities going for it. One is that it be immediately accessible, not too much room for nuances or subtlety. And that it be entertaining, that it has to work for a house, you have to be entertained. Do you see any kind of limitation in this type of poetry?

M.A.: No. I think all poetry should be entertaining and the subtleties come in as they are needed. I've only read you poems from the first section of the anthology which is the outlaw section. These poems work with those two qualities and they are accessible. They've got a story-line, and they come straight at you. It's not investigating the self in a very personal way, necessarily. Instead, I think they're involved in establishing conditions and complaints about the environment. They are poems that display anger. The first poems, the three poems I've read, are all from a section called "Outlaw Poetry."

Q: I was just reading this thing John Ciardi said about

good poetry having more verbs than it has adjectives. Do
you think so?

M.A.: Yes. I like verbs. They're action. Were you hearing a
lot of adjectives?

Q: Well, I could imagine street poetry being full of adjectives. Sounding down people's mothers would be a lot of adjectives. That's a form of street poetry, and that has a lot of
adjectives.

M.A.: Yes, but the successful thing is that it's the kind of
street confrontation where you have to rhyme your stuff
right quick. That's terrific exercise, by the way, and it always depends on your verb, on what you have your mother
doing. The humor is in the verb.

Q: It seemed like this was verb-y poetry that you were
reading.

M.A.: That's good.

Q: I remember it seemed that the theatrical side of your
work had gotten a little bit to Lucky, too much, in a way,
like he'd walk around in his apartment day and night
shouting out words at the walls as if he was speaking to
somebody. And I showed him some poetry by Mayakovsky,
he looked at two pages and said I'm not into reading poetry,
I *write* poetry, which was a bit much.

M.A.: Well, you have readers, and you have a lot of writers
that are not readers, that are not accurate readers, and that's
just that situation with reading skills. Your statement brings
me to my third point.

III

READING: ORAL MEMORY, READING
VERSUS TAPE RECORDER AND PLEASURE

I like to read, but a lot of people don't. Miky is a terrific
reader, and the reason for that is that time in jail is time for
reading. But he is on the streets now, and you won't catch
him reading unless it's a book by a friend of his. So I think

it's a matter of conditioning. Bobbie Louise was talking about this earlier. She said that she was lucky she had discovered reading as a pleasureable experience before she got into reading as a cultural identity, or something—what was it you said?

B.L.H.: I could read anything I wanted to read, and I read everything I could get my hands on, so I had the experience of reading before I got to that place where they spend the first two or three years in school teaching you to read. Thereafter, reading begins to be applied. And the point at which it's an avocation, most persons run an enormous risk of being kicked out of shape. Instead of being cut loose by reading, reading is used as a constraining factor. It maintains the status quo. We're directed toward certain readings, kinds of thought exchange. I learned to read really fast. I knew I'd read for pleasure.

M.A.: That's great. I remember my mother taught me how to read. I read for pleasure before it became a symbol of being acculturated. I think people's pleasure in reading is destroyed by public schooling that makes reading into a horrible experience. But I think that as the years go on, pleasure in reading grows.

B.L.H.: Is that nine-year-old kid [Georgie Lopez] learning to read and write from the situation he's in with you?

M.A.: Now, yes. He can read and write, but not through the school. That's the terror of it. We had a fourteen year old, Hector Rodriguez, who couldn't read or write.

What we did was to talk the idea of his play out to Miguel Piñero who worked on it with Hector. The play was produced at the Theater Genesis, directed by Tito Goya and was picked up by NBC. It was televised and it got Hector a nomination for an Emmy.

B.L.H.: Did they know he was fourteen?

M.A.: Yes, they knew he was fourteen. That was *Lonely Lives* and the other play that was produced with *Lonely Lives* was *'Hoe Stroll.*

QUESTION: So the kids or adults that are poets without

being able to read or write, learn everything just by ear, then.

M.A.: Yes. Poetry is an oral tradition.

Q: It blows my mind totally.

M.A.: Well, poetry is an oral tradition. I think that before this democratic idea of educating everybody, the poet was responsible for telling interesting oral stories. This responsibility was very real then. Poetry is oral and the ear works wonders on language. You don't have to know how to write or read it. It's *preferable* in this society, but you don't have to. *Lonely Lives* is a beautifully structured play with a middle, a beginning, and an end. Hector worked it out with Miguel Piñero. Joe Papp's secretary typed out *'Hoe Stroll.*

Papp fell in love with Hector's energies and made his secretary available to him. In fact, Hector wrote four plays during that period. But you see, it's all ear. Writers who write from just the ear overcome a lot of problems that surface with writers who have been coming to writing through the structures of grammar and through the rhetorical raps about what is proper to do with language.

B.L.H.: Most of the writers I know learned writing through reading. And that means that they've been reading, when they realize there's such a thing as good writing, as opposed to bad writing. You can latch on to somebody you think's a really good writer and read everything of that person's. As soon as you get into that kind of discrimination, you're taking it back through the eyes, you're in an immediate superego problem. You're in that canopy problem, where there's this weight over you, namely, the experience of writing through your eyes, and now you're looking at what you're doing and you've got this problem of what all that stuff was, and how somebody else did it. Whereas if you're taking it off, if you're writing it the way you'd say it, you suddenly find that you're cut loose to the extent that your mind can be in a general conversation, as opposed to making it work on the page—which is immediately a problem that stands between you and it.

M.A.: Hector memorized his plays and one of the inter-

esting things is that he was proving to people on the street
that he could read by taking his play out and reading. But
only because he had memorized it. We tried to deal with
that by telling him that now he had to do that with other
people's work, to be able to read it too. But he could read
his own work, and that was plenty for him. That's how we
got a whole *Romeo and Juliet* on the Lower East Side, directed by Richard August. We were going crazy. The kids
couldn't read Shakespeare, but the tape recorder turned out
to be a friend. Richard August taped the whole role for
each person. Then they would take it home with them and
play it at home. The next day our Romeo came back with
all his monologues memorized. Oral transmission is the most
direct. And memory relates to radio and TV faster than it
does to the printed page. We performed *Romeo and Juliet*
for Peter Brooke. He walked up to Juliet and said, "you're
real." Juliet was fourteen and Romeo was fifteen and it
looked real. They were beautiful to look at and it was all
working. They couldn't read Shakespeare on the page, but
they could pick it off the tape. You have got to go where you
have to go when the problem is literacy.

Q: I see that a lot of the poetry you've been reading and
poetry that came out of the ghetto, whatever you want to
call it, as a reaction against capitalism and the training that
capitalism puts on people through education and through
schools, when the schools don't work. It's harder to fight
back against it using the medium that they were trying to
teach, which would be words, and writing. I wonder how
you see poetry that is of use, that is definitely trying to do
something, like to raise consciousness, or whatever, that's
coming out of here, and how you see that as compared to
most of everything else that's published in the United
States.

M.A.: That's a hard question. Some of the poetry in the
Nuyorican Poetry Anthology is about capitalism in a very
obvious way. In the first section of the Anthology, the Outlaw Poetry section, the poetry is a complaint and a direct aggression, like throwing down the glove. In the second

section, the poetry changes. It goes into what I call Evolu-
tionary. That means the poet is scoping himself in a violent
situation and is trying to see what to do to adjust the situation so that he can survive. So, the second section is an adjustment, and the poetry constantly changes. It goes into
seeing the self and analyzing it so that the self can adjust
and not just be in direct confrontation, not just be responding with aggression to aggression. The third section of the
book is called "Dusmic," which is a word Moses Figueroa
made up. It means that the poetry in the Dusmic section
catches the poet trying to respond to aggression by
converting it into his strength. That's a more difficult
process to describe, but the poetry in that section is literally
trying to confront aggression and convert it into strength.
Just how that is done, I don't know. The same poet that in
section one might be screaming against capitalism and
against racism, is in the third section in a more contemplative mood, seeing himself deal with that aggression by
understanding and making it work for him. So the work in
the Anthology has many moods.

Q: Well, what poetry traditions are there, you know, New
York being the largest Puerto Rican city in the world?

M.A.: It's an oral tradition. Let me establish the point this
way. The average Puerto Rican kid who cannot read or
write has one or two poems in Spanish that he can quote to
you. These are passed down by the family. For example, in
my artillery there are seven poems that come from
childhood. Way before I learned to read or write I could recite them. The relationship between the oral poetic tradition and the people is very healthy. The only thing that
they don't know is that they have to pay me for being poet.
I'll answer you about Puerto Ricans in New York. I don't
live in Puerto Rico. The relationship between the poet and
the New York Puerto Rican is healthy in that they need
him. They need to hear his voice. They need to hear his
rap. They have to listen to him because his voice compels attention. Now, they are not yet paying the poet, that is, there
is no habit of buying poetry books.

Sources

ALGARIN, MIGUEL and PIÑERO, MIGUEL, eds., *Nuyorican Poetry: An Anthology of Puerto Rican Words and Feelings* (New York: Morrow, 1975). Freeee that Sister" (*Lolita Lebron . . . Mandamos*) © 1975 by Lucky CienFuegos; "The Sounds of Sixth Street" © 1975 by Martita Morales; "The Book of Genesis according to Saint Miguelito" © 1975 by Miguel Piñero; "About the Rats" (*About los Ratones*) © 1975 by Jorge Lopez. Reprinted by permission of the publisher.

Photo by Phil Schaafsma

Lewis MacAdams

POETRY AND POLITICS

JULY 3, 1975

"About three o'clock this morning I was leaning against a
wall at the Emerson apartments, at Naropa Institute, and
suddenly I thought about the people who had given me the
world; I had this flash of sheer panic. I said I'm going to try
to tell everybody everything, so forgive me. I'd like to dedi-
cate this talk to two of my teachers, Bob Creeley and Jack
Clarke from the University of Buffalo and to Jack Boyce, a
painter and carpenter and now dead—because he is the man
who taught me to build a fire."

—Lewis MacAdams

I WANT TO talk about William Yeats and Ezra Pound and
Charles Olson, and I want to talk about politics—theirs and
mine and yours. I will start with a poem from Charles Olson's third volume of *Maximus Poems,* called *Added to
Making a Republic in Gloom at Watchhouse Point.* This is
what Olson says:

> An actual earth of value to
> construct one, from rhythm to
> image, and image is knowing, and
> knowing, Confucius says, brings one

to the goal:
Nothing is possible without doing it.
It is where the test lies.

And another quote from Thomas Jefferson: "The revolution took place in the minds of the people."

I live in a town about thirty miles north of San Francisco, and five years ago last winter two oil tankers collided under the Golden Gate Bridge in a fog, and spilled hundreds of thousands of gallons of bunker oil, which is thick and viscous, almost like coal-tar. Most of this great blob mass of oil floated on the water's surface, floating north with the currents, out the Golden Gate and up the coast toward Bolinas.

Bolinas is one of the only lagoons left on the California coast as the home for thousands of birds, and it's a stop for many thousands of other birds on journeys up and down the Pacific Flyway. A lagoon is very loveable to birds because of its mix of salt water and fresh, so what grows there for birds, stuff like pickleweed and ghost shrimp, makes the lagoon very rich. The lagoon is a breeding ground for egrets and herons too; and as the oil came slowly up the coast toward it, the town seemed to spontaneously organize around this event.

Standard Oil sent out their hirelings with the heavy equipment, which they ended up using to bury the blobs of oil. But of course for dealing with the oil at sea, there was nothing they could do, and for keeping the oil out of the lagoon, they brought out this little yellow string of pontoons which instantly flipped over when the five-knot current in the channel at the lagoon's mouth hit it.

I don't know if you've ever seen a bird when it's covered with bunker oil, but it's sort of like a napalmed child. Its body temperature goes up and up as it struggles with the oil, until finally, death. And thousands of shorebirds and seals and shellfish and starfish died in this holocaust, and out of the death grew a town sense of awareness that crystallized as a doorbell-ringing, survey-taking, political organization called the Bolinas Future Studies Center; I was one member. The Future Studies Center struck on a single obvious issue: the Board of the Public Utilities District, the water and sewer board, was in the process of organizing the community on behalf of a large bond issue to build a sewer for the whole Bolinas downtown and mesa, most of which was land that had never been sewered.

They wanted to collect all the shit and water and treat it, sock some chlorine to it and dump it out to sea. And that seemed totally insane. We just started by saying, "Why?" and after awhile we had to learn, "Well, why not?" We began to study, none of us had any particular background in this—one person was an electrician, another raised children, another worked part-time as a night watchman, another was a dreamer, I was a poet, and another studied apes. It was everybody learning about sewerage. What it was, really, Shit and Water mostly, not Waste: two very valuable resources when treated wisely. One thing led to another and we elected our own people to the water board. We stopped the original sewerage system from being built and replaced it with a much smaller system which serves only the houses already on sewers (downtown—the rest of the town uses septic tanks) , and built what is now called Sewer Farm—a series of ponds which aerates the shit-water over a period of months, and then we spray the water on to fields which are leased out to grow different kinds of hay by local farmers. In the course of this time I was appointed to the Water Board, to fill a term when somebody resigned, and then I was elected to the Utilities District for real, four months later.

Now what does a poet do on a water board? Well, first of all, obviously, you do what there is to do. Everybody on the board was very activist, and we were even paid a little, so we each had certain functions, responsibilities, and my first job was to oversee the rebuilding of the road up to our little dams on Arroyo Hondo, the Bolinas water source. I got up there, and I could barely read the engineers drawings, so obviously my first task was to learn, and I was standing there shaking my head, and then the head of the maintenance crew handed me this big wrench and asked me to help him at the dam, and I found myself walking along with this wrench and it's like I've just been handed the fascicles that rule Rome—you know, the actual tools of government. The keys to the water system are the actual tools of government, just as the now-ceremonial "keys to the city" were once used to open the city's gates. But it's also A WRENCH. So I learned what to do.

When I was on the water board, in addition to the everyday deciding about a new filter, and writing the Utility District Newsletter, I found myself thinking about words a lot. Words like "Development." And how that word got turned—at least where I live—to mean something very bad. Like, Oh he's a *developer,* and I felt like I wanted to cleanse that word. Or "Sewerage." I wanted to make that more familiar and at the same time useful. So when it came time to order the sign for the new sewer system we were designing, I insisted, over the Federal Government's (who were paying for most of the system) objections, and over the demurrers of my allies on the water board, who didn't really care—that the sign at the construction site say not Sewerage Treatment Facility like it does nearly everywhere in the U.S. where the Clean Water Acts of Congress pay for the work, but Sewerage Resource System. I wanted the sign to say what we were actually gonna do. And that sign is still standing there today catching the eyes of passers-by, with information for their own use. And that's why I am a poet. Amen.

Anyway, I wanted to establish these facts of politics with you, because I say that the three poets Yeats, Pound, and Olson also involved themselves politically, and I want to discuss their political-poetical work today.

I'll start with another quote from Olson, from Letter Six of *The Maximus Poems:*

> Polis
> Is Eyes.

And I want to hit you with another quote, a long one from Ezra Pound's translation of Confucius:

> The men of old wanting to clarify and diffuse throughout the empire that light which comes from looking straight into the heart and then acting, first set up good government in their own states; wanting good government in their own states, they first established order in their own families; wanting order in the home, they first disciplined themselves; desiring self-discipline, they rectified their own hearts; and wanting to rectify their hearts, they sought precise verbal definitions of their inarticulate thoughts, the tones given off by the heart.

> From the emperor, Son of Heaven, to the common man, singly and all together, self-discipline is the root.

> If the root be in confusion, nothing will be well-governed.

My definition of politics definitely rises from Olson's, my working, *acting* definition of politics (because I've come to think of myself as a political man) is that politics grows from the center out. Visionary politics is the same as practical politics, how you make your world.

In my world, land quickly becomes a passion. How do you dwell on this planet? I don't mean localism, either—"This is the best little 'ol town in the U. S. of A." I mean, this is a small planet, and it's a local solar system. It's like Wendell Berry says, "What I stand for is what I stand on." Of course, the sewer needs new pipes sometimes, and you work at that if you can, and I can. But we are also in and of SPACE. I remember Jack Boyce, the painter, telling the State Highway Department people, at a public meeting on whether to widen the road across Mt. Tamalpais—"First of all, it's a sacred mountain." Second of all, one can not be carried away by passion, which leads endlessly to the "isms." I asked William Burroughs, what did he think the most dangerous words in the language were. And he said, any word that ends in ism: Communism, Capitalism, Idealism. And I asked, "Well, do you think there is any such thing as a just ruler?"

And he said, "What do you mean, *just?* What's just for the judge is not necessarily just for the criminal." And I realized that perhaps my mistake was in using the word ruler, because I really mean leader. I quote Burroughs as a Cautionary. I am not talking about being swept away with enthusiasm, but there are leaders. There are different leaders for different tasks. There's a war chief and there's a dance chief. There's maybe a business chief (Is the President of the United States the business chief?) and there are "religious" chiefs. Or maybe the business chief is the Hunt Chief in America. In any case, there are no hierarchies.

Yeats, Pound, and Olson, how did they see and seek political change, what did they actually do? Well, first of all, they wrote poems. It is first of all as poets that they guide me. Their words guide their deeds.

After the Irish Revolution, after Southern Ireland freed itself from Great Britain, when the first Irish Parliament was called, in 1922, Yeats was appointed to a six-year term as Senator. The Irish Parliament was divided into an elected and an appointed house, and Yeats was appointed by President Cosgrave for his service to the Irish Revolution and for his greatness as a man of letters, for his plays and poems in praise of heroism, plays like *Cathleen Ni Houlihand,* and poems like *Easter 1916:*

> All Changed, Changed Utterly,
> A terrible beauty is born

Poems like this one, written on the instant where one decides where one stands, or where we see, as Yeats said in *The Circus Animals Desertion,* "character isolated by a deed," are truly great.

The day Yeats was appointed to the Senate, he cast a horoscope for the Irish Free State and for himself as Senator. He found the portents positive for himself, but violent and unstable for the new nation. As soon as Ireland was partitioned, civil war began in Ireland. The I.R.A. and its supporters felt that anyone who served in the new government was acquiescing to the permanent partition of the country, and many of Yeats' closest friends' homes and libraries were bombed and burned in the years that followed. We can find in Yeats' last poems a very cynical and embittered view of politics, viz: *The Great Day:*

> Hurrah for revolution and more cannon-shot!
> A beggar upon horseback lashes a beggar on foot.

Or finally, his reply to Thomas Mann, who was saying in those days leading up to World War II, "In our time the destiny of man presents its meaning in political terms." Yeat's answer to Mann was his poem *Politics,* where he acknowledges the pull on him, perhaps of "war and war's alarms." But stronger than that is the pull toward nostalgia and love—"O that I were young again and held her in my arms."

Yet in Yeats' work in the Irish Senate he actually accomplished something—"the slow, exciting work," Yeats called it in his Senate Speeches, "of creating institutions." A few years ago the University of Indiana published a collection of Yeats' political speeches. When you read them you find that while Yeats had a considerably higher than average senate attendance record, he didn't make a lot of speeches. When he did speak though, he knew what he was talking about. He fought against censorship of books and films, helped set up Ireland's copyright laws, and spoke up often on the subject of education. In fact, he made himself an expert on the Irish educational system by traveling around the country for several years looking at the schools.

In a speech on educational philosophy in 1925, Yeats said, "Begin geography with your native fields, arithmetic by counting the school chairs and measuring the walls, history with local monuments, religion with the local saints; and then pass on from that to the nation itself." That Yeats worked with his own poetry while he served the nation is evident from his great poem *Among School Children,* written out of his experiences inspecting Ireland's schools. I've got to read it to you because it's so beautiful.

Yeats' other solid political work while he was a senator included heading the committee that chose the designs for Ireland's beautiful coinage, choosing the design for judges' costumes that were eventually accepted by the nation, and leading the fight to have the great Hugh Lane collection of modern French painting returned to Dublin from England. He wrote the Irish Senate's official recommendations for the collection cataloguing and translation of the ancient Gaelic and Irish texts.

Perhaps most important, Yeats led the fight to legalize divorce and remarriage in the free state. He prophesied that arms would never reunite Ireland, but that if the Protestants were not alienated and frightened away by legal and social codes which were totally Catholic, they would eventually accept Ireland as their country too. Yeats took from the Irish philosopher Burke the idea that "the state is a tree, not a mechanism to be pulled in pieces and put up again, but an oak tree that had grown through centuries." Yeats was allied in many ways with the conservative land-owning gentry wing of the Irish Senate, but his positions were always independent and his speeches without cant. At the end of his six-year term, leaving active political life, he said in his last senate speech, "I think we should not lose sight of the simple fact that it is more desirable and more important to have able men in this House than representative men in this house." After he left office he told his secretary, Ezra Pound, as quoted from the Senate Speeches, "Neither you, nor I, nor any other of our excitable profession can match these old lawyers, old bankers, old business men, who, because all habit and memory, have begun to rule the world." Twenty years later, Pound's response came in the form of *Canto LXXX*, from Pound's detention cage in Pisa:

> If a man don't occasionally sit in a senate
>   how can he pierce the dark mind of a senator.

One wonders at the tone in which Yeats advised Pound. Was it that Yeats thought that politics was beneath an artist, or was it that Yeats saw that Pound, of all people, should steer clear because of his ideas or ways? In either case, the example of Pound as politician and poet is most perplexing. Pound spent his entire life obsessed with structure, and the need to reform and educate America: "The Thought of what America would be like," he wrote, "if the classics had a wider circulation. Ah. it troubles my sleep." Yet Pound ended up at the end of World War II the only American civilian charged with treason against the United States, charged with treason for acting as a radio propagandist for the Italian monarchy during the war. Pound was captured after the American invasion and brought to an American military prison in Pisa, where he was held in a specially built steel cage in the middle of the prison yard, without furniture or writing materials. Let us consider the great poet in his sixtieth year, huddled under dusty blankets in his cage, floodlights trained on him all night, bearing the stares of curious G.I.s walking by each day on their way to chow, as Pound lay there with the one book he was allowed to have—a Chinese language text of the writings of Confucius. Let us consider this, poets, and beware. Be aware and be clear!

It is impossible to ignore the scurrilously racist nature of parts of Pound's *Cantos,* and of his radio addresses; and in fact in his later years, Pound remarked that he felt the *Cantos* and his life a failure because of his "suburban anti-semitism." But there is so much beauty and good sense in the *Cantos,* that it would be silly not to read them. Pound's politics are rooted in Confucius. He writes in *Canto CXVI,* "if love be not in the house there is nothing," and that is where I constantly have to remind myself to begin. From heart and home our vision—my vision—inevitably expands to the country, to the land mass currently called America.

And it's to the *Cantos*—by his own insistence, a failure—that I look for the political themes I find useful and important today. One of the themes that recur in the *Cantos* is an

examination of the influences of Thomas Jefferson and John
Adams. As Pound points out, Jefferson was a creator, the inventor of America. But Adams was a man who concerned
himself with the ongoing political structures that are necessary for an idea-nature—or, as Robin Blaser calls it, an
image-nation—to survive. And as we dig America in the
Seventies, and see the need for a government based on the
consciousness of balance, we have to conceive of a socio-
political structure not based, as it has been for the last two
hundred years, on physical growth. Because the growth of
America has been based, as Adams saw, on a system which
Pound calls Usury, the system where money, or debt, becomes the basis of government, and where multi-national
corporations, with no roots but in the shift of supply, control
finance. The poet John Thorpe has pointed out that for every 200 dollars an American was earning in 1973, 70 dollars
was going to repay the national debt, and that debt is owed
to private corporations. And the very junk these
corporations produce (the International Telephone and
Telegraph Company produces more than half of America's
sickeningly distorted "white" breads) is the confirmation of
Pound's lines from *Canto XLV,* "The Usura Canto,"
published forty years ago:

> with usura, sin against nature,
> is thy bread ever more of stale rags,

Pound went into anger, enraged I think at his inability to
affect change with his words. But a poet cannot afford that
rage, to be that locked-in to time. The works must grow
patiently, the poet cannot stand next to his nation, like a
doctor with a thermometer, measuring his own effect. In any
case, the final *Cantos* he produced in his lifetime are
marked by a beautiful patience, as this example of *Canto
CXVI* shows.

> i.e. it coheres all right
> even if my notes do no cohere

After his incarceration at Pisa, Pound was returned to the United States where he was immediately put into St. Elizabeth's Hospital in Washington, D.C., while the government waited trial to figure out what to do with him. Psychiatrists testified for and against him, newspapers accused him of pulling a Rudolf Hess, poets made their stand. (Wallace Stephens against Pound, by the way. And William Carlos Williams lost his chance for the chair as poet of the Library of Congress because of a Jacob Javits-led attack on Williams as being the friend of Pound.) At his sanity hearing, The New York Herald Tribune reported (February 14, 1946), "Psychiatrists reported that nearly two months' observation of Pound's mental condition revealed a number of 'fixed ideas' held by the poet: that his mission in life was to save the United States Constitution, that the only way to world peace was through the teachings of Confucius, that he could have prevented the formation of the Axis and the war by uniting intellectual groups of the world and that he was persecuted by bureaucrats."

The federal government finally decided that Pound was not mentally fit to stand trial and returned him to St. Elizabeth's, where he spent the next ten years. But the government held the treason charge over him for thirteen years (there is no statute of limitations on treason), until he was permitted to leave St. Elizabeth's and return to Italy. In 1948 Dorothy Pound brought out of St. Elizabeth's a three-page letter she had typed to Pound's dictation, which was printed in *The Trial of Ezra Pound*. In it Pound states, "E.P. was not a propagandist in the pay of a foreign government, he has not betrayed America but tried to prevent America from betraying Mother Europa." Michael Wolfe told me that Pound himself had pinpointed only two instances in Northern Hemisphere civilizations—one in ancient China, and one for 150 years in a city-state in Italy—of a kind of economy existing where money was considered the common tool of all the people, where it could be drawn on by need, and where all human labor was in a sense the interest we pay for having bodies. These are certainly fleeting instances in recorded time, but who among us is to say that Pound was wrong for having committed all to his vision?

When Pound was in St. Elizabeth's, he had many visitors. One man who came often to visit Pound, and afterwards certainly claimed Pound's influence, was John Kaspar. Kaspar gained his greatest fame with his speeches rousing white mobs to riot against the integration of Little Rock Central High School in 1954. The whole story of Pound's trial is in the book of his defense lawyer Julien Cornell, *The Trial of Ezra Pound*.

Another visitor to Ezra Pound was Charles Olson, the poet who was at that time working in Washington for the administration of Franklin Roosevelt, or "Frankie the perjurer," as Pound referred to him in the letter quoted above. Of the three poets we are talking about, Olson's politics are the most familiar to me, the politics most rooted in the reality of the day-to-day. During the early days of the Second World War, Olson, who had previously been a mailman and a long-time graduate student, went to work for Alan Cranston in the Office of War Information. I think he became the Assistant Chief of the O.W.I., specializing in press releases to raise the spirits of the Polish-Americans and other European-Americans whose countries were at war. A special affinity with the Poles must have been evident because, according to George Butterick of the Olson Archives at the University of Connecticut Library, Olson was asked by the Poles to represent them at the early meetings of the emerging United Nations Security Council. But the Western-oriented "free Pole" faction was defeated, and they had no further demands for Charles Olson's services. Olson's work with the Office of War Information led him to work in 1944 with the Democratic National Committee, preparing the ethnic-American voting strategy. Butterick has at the Olson Archives a memo from Olson to Roosevelt, urging the President to pay more attention to Polish-American interests. Olson quit Democratic Party politics in 1944, just before the death of Roosevelt, but was back in '48 at the Democratic Convention in Philadelphia helping Claude

Pepper from Florida try to stop the nomination of Harry
Truman. Olson told Butterick that just as a delegate stood
up to nominate Pepper, there was suddenly a power black-
out at the Convention, and the meeting was unable to go on.
That was the end of Olson's partisan political work, but anyone who knows Olson's *Maximus Poems,* or the last poems
in *Archaeologist of Morning,* knows his continuous involvement with the Gloucester City Council, as well as with a total consciousness of politics. "Polis" Olson says again, "is
eyes."

> I am a ward
> and precinct
> man myself and hate
> universalization

> I believe in religion not magic or science I believe in
> society as religious both man and society as religious.

Which are for me true words, and as I quoted Olson at the
beginning of this paper, "Nothing is possible without doing
it."

Last night I found myself at the Bolinas Stinson School
Board Budget Meeting, and when a program that I believed
in very much was cut from the budget on ideological
grounds, but with the pretense of "expense," I found myself
calling a member of the School Board a lying motherfucker,
and in the shock of silence in the room I listened to my
heart pound, abashed for a few moments, appalled at what
I'd done, and then I realized yes, that man *is* lying. So I said
it to him again. The fact that he didn't jump over the table
and hit me gave me time to think back to an earlier, more
boring part of the meeting, when I was doodling in my note-
book trying to figure out how to finish this talk on poetry
and politics with what I believed; i.e., how poetry and
politics intertwines in me like a plant growing, turning on
its stalk, so that its whole being has its chance to reach the
sun.

Mao says that reality is the starting place; so to start with,

I have to say that I believe class struggle is only *one* of the
realities in this world. So when I hear the world totally
described in those terms I get bored. I feel that the body
politic includes all beings in the universe invented in all
forms, and that politics, to be accurate, must reflect and deal
with that. Since at least the Judaeo-Christian era began, we
have lived in a kind of human racism, a pyramidal vision of
the earth with the humans at the top, and all other creatures
placed here, somehow, to serve us from below. To displace
this human self-definition is as important today as it was
several hundred years ago. To revise the notion that the sun
revolves around the earth. It is one of the most important
struggles of our time.

To go further, to make this more personal, I want to say
Life is an adventure; every serious challenge along the path
is an opportunity. I am totally confused about love, wish
only the best for all men and women, and hope that the
sexual politics of our time will bring us to more knowledge.
When it's time to dance, it's time to dance, and there are
people who lead and *call* the dance. When it's time to fight,
we have to be warriors, prepared for anything, at all times
alert; at any second all bets are off, each being has to bring
to bear all he or she has, to be present. I like what Bob
Creeley says, which we put in as an epigraph at the beginning of the Bolinas Plan, now part of the Marin County
General Plan: "The plan is the body." And I believe what
Olson says in the last Maximus Volume:

> I believe in God
> as fully physical

And I understand what Olson means by a human universe.
"It is a human universe," says poet Ted Berrigan in his
book *The Sonnets,* "and I is a correspondant."

As I got deeper and deeper into this talk, I found myself
looking for Yeats' and Pound's and Olson's last words on
politics, how they summed it up; and I read among Olson's
last words, these again from the *Maximus Poems:*

There is now no break in the
future, a thing does flow etc. and
intensity
is the characteristic throughout
the system.

Politics is the precision with which we live our lives.
"Politics is eyes," Olson says, and I'm looking. Since the beginning of his first term I have been observing as carefully
as I could the words and actions of the Governor of
California, Jerry Brown. What poets know and hucksters
tend to forget is that words are at the root of our sight, and
that words are at the root of our societies. The chief role of
the leaders of our societies is to state the terms, the tones of
the general reality. That is, what becomes the laws. Leaders
are real, the world, though it is the ultimate illusion, is real
also. In vetoing the state senate bill reinstating the death
penalty in California, Governor Brown wrote in *The San
Francisco Chronicle,* "Ultimately each of us must decide for
ourselves what kind of world he or she wants to live in."

Many of you here are poets and writers, people who
measure carefully your words and deeds. I would like to
take this opportunity to endorse Jerry Brown for President
of the United States and urge all of you to study Jerry
Brown's words and acts and see if you can support him too.

The revolution of consciousness that we are both
progenitors and victims of has shown us the physical fallacy
of representation. That is, nobody represents us, but us. But
just as we know the meaning of networks, which is the
world we share with others employed like ourselves, many
of us have gained at least the inkling of a need to recognize
our places in a society that we were born to be part of, and
our responsibility to change or maintain the world that we
share. By bringing greater clarity to the role of governor of
California, Jerry Brown has inevitably brought a greater
clarity to the public part of our lives. "Legislators," says
Brown, "are the unacknowledged poets of the world." Yeats,
Pound, and Olson were all men who moved in the world

and moved the world, because they knew that both what they said and did mattered, and that words and deeds are empty without each other. Poetry and politics are one.

Thank you.

Sources

CORNELL, JULIAN, *The Trial of Ezra Pound* (New York: John Day Co., 1966), pp. 107–109.

BERRIGAN, TED, "Sonnet LII," *The Sonnets,* (New York: Grove Press).

OLSON, CHARLES, *Maximus Poems: Volume Three* (New York: Viking Press, 1960), Maximus 3, Letter 6, pp. 11, 13, 55, 190, and 225. Reprinted by permission of the publisher.

POUND, EZRA, *Confucious* (New York: New Directions, 1951, 1970), pp. 29-31, 33.

POUND, EZRA, *Pisan Cantos* (New York: New Directions, 1940), Canto XLV, p. 229; Canto LXXX, p. 25 (Senate Speeches); and Canto CXVI, p. 797.

PEARCE, DONALD R., ed., *Senate Speeches of Yeats* (Bloomington, Indiana: Indiana University Press, 1960), No. 11, p. 11; No. 14, pp. 151-152; and No. 15, p. 25.

YEATS, W.B., *Collected Poems of W.B. Yeats* (New York: MacMillan Pub. Co., 1974), p. 178, 336, 309, and 337.

Photo by Rachel Homer

Ed Sanders

INVESTIGATIVE POETRY:
THE CONTENT OF HISTORY
WILL BE POETRY

JULY 8, 1975

*REVISED IN THE FALL OF 1975,
AND THE WINTER OF 1976*

> There is no end
> to *Gnosis:*
>
> The hunger
> for *DATA*

A

THE GOAL: an era of investigative poesy wherein one can be controversial, radical, and not have the civilization rise up to smite down the bard. To establish and to maintain it. POETS MAY REMAIN IN THE RADIX, UNCOM-PROMISING, REVOLUTIONARY, SEDITIOUS, ABSO-LUTE.

> POET as Investigator
> Interpreter of Sky Froth
> Researcher of the Abyss

Human Universer
Prophet
Prophet without death
as a consequence

My statement is this: that poetry, to go forward, in my view, has to begin a voyage into the description of *historical reality.*

Last winter I was examining the text, and the history of the composition, of Hart Crane's *The Bridge,* and I was struck by the historical scholarship the poet had undertaken in the five or so years he labored in its composition. Crane consulted numerous books on American history, building a ziggurat of scholarship with which, as the poet intended, *The Bridge* might confront the dry neo-Pindarian puritan sonorities of the *Wasteland,* which much of *The Bridge* was intended to confront.

In addition, for 15 years I had followed the work and career of Charles Olson, particularly the *Maximus Poems,* and the poems contained in that Grove Press book, *The Distances,* and was always amazed how Charles, with his enormous intellect and energy, was able, by consulting old city files—that is, books and documents relating to a formerly obscure New England fishing settlement, Gloucester, Massachusetts—to transform these researches into high-order poetry, using his principles of *composition by field* as enumerated in his projective verse manifesto, the result being poetry as history, or history-poesy, or Clio come down to Gloucester in a breeze of High Energy Verse Grids, or Data Clusters, a form of poetic presentation I will discuss in greater detail later.

And then there is the matter of *Howl.* When *Howl* was published in the '50's, it was accepted for what it was, a religious document of great beauty and awesome threnodic power, and a work, we were rightly certain, destined to change American history. Its IMPLICATIONS were historical. As years went by, and the analysis of the poem continued, I time-tracked the poem's implications as they oozed into the historical life-style plexus. So doing, I came to greater and greater awareness of the poet's investigative techniques.

That is, *Howl,* with its wonderful fresh combinations of ancient Greek metres combined with long held-breath lines lasting, in some cases, 5 to 10 seconds, is a work of American history. I remember this spring reading a book called *The Beat Book,* published by Arthur and Glee Knight; particularly the interview with Carl Solomon, who relates in that great Solomonian mode, how Ginsberg was always, in the classic gum-shoe, or muse-sandal, manner, asking oodles of questions of his friends, clarifying anecdotes, keeping files on all his friends, many of which anecdotes and data-files turning up later on in *Howl.* In fact, from an examination of the anecdotes in *Howl,* we may devolve one of the first rules of Investigative Poetry: Do not hesitate to open up a case file on a friend.

A good example is the famous Mallarmé potato salad toss, immortalized by the bard on page 15 of the City Lights edition of *Howl and other Poems:*

> who threw potato salad at CCNY lecturers on Dada-
> ism and subsequently presented themselves on the
> granite steps of the madhouse with shaven heads
> and harlequin speech of suicide, demanding instant
> lobotomy . . .

In the interview in *The Beat Book,* Solomon confirms the historicity of such a 'tato-toss, but corrects the poetic license of the poem by pointing out that the salad hurling, performed by Solomon and several friends, rather than oc-curing during a lecture on Dadaism, occurred in the course of a lecture on Mallarmé given by Wallace Markfield.

B. INVESTIGATIVE ELEUTHERARCHS

Lawyers have a term: "to make law." You "make law" when you're involved in a case or an appeal which, as in Supreme

Court decisions which have expanded the scope of personal freedom, opens up new human avenues.

You make law.

Bards, in a similar way, "make reality," or, really, they "make freedom" or they create new modes of what we might term Eleutherarchy, or the dance of freedom.

C. THE LEGACY OF EZRA POUND

Purist Distillations from the Data-Midden: the essence of Investigative Poetry: Lines of lyric beauty descend from the data clusters.

The Cantos of Ezra Pound first gave us melodic blizzards of data-fragments. History as slime-sift for morality; Olson grew out of that Poundian concern. I don't personally believe an Investigative Poet has to research *The Cantos* for clues to the future. More of the mode of futurity might be learned by studying Pound's *Confucian Odes,* certainly some of the most beautiful and varied melodies anyone has written. On the other hand, who can deny the didactically overpowering drill-job that Canto 45, or 81, performed upon our unsuspecting brows. I remember hitchhiking around the country in the late '50's, the only books in my pack, besides *Buddhist Texts Through the Ages,* being *Howl,* D. Thomas's *Collected Poems,* Kant's *Prolegomenon to Any Future Metaphysics,* and *The Cantos.* And it was *The Cantos* that trapped one forever in its warp.

Pound gave us shaped texts: some of his pages, such as 81, and, say 75 (Out of Phlegethon!), and many to be found even by a quick spiffle through the pages: THESE PAGES, IN CONSIDERATION OF THEIR SHAPE AND AR-RANGEMENTS OF DATA-GRIDS, ARE OF BEAUTY. That is, Pound helped verse escape the dungeon of the column inch.

And Pound was a skilled collagist: and the lesson is this: that an Investigative Poet of any worth at all will have to become as skilled a collagist as the early Braque.

The poetry of *The Cantos* would emerge, as it were, from a plexus of memories, quote-torrents from the Greek, Latin, Italian, Chinese, French, Arabic, Egyptian, *et al.,* from quick historical vignettes, even, like, newspaper headlines, whereupon, on a sudden, flash! the essence appears; an exquisite line begins and a cadence of purest verse thrills the eye-brain.

Thus Olson, thus Ginsberg, thus Investigative Poetry.

> The fault of Pound's epic, in my opinion, is that it races too near the course of Achilles, of war lords, of patriarchial death-breaths. And it speaks, in my opinion, too strongly in favor of a society run by austere whip-freaks and fascists, and it condones Hitlerism and anti-Semitism.

> On the other hand, Pound's insight into the money-hallucinated-out-of-nothing nature of the banking system, where sleazisms like David Rockefeller can create money by whim, has been an inspiration to many a poor poet trying to scrounge up even a quarter to buy an egg-cream at Gem Spa's.

And the important lesson we can learn from Pound, in the matter of writing investigative poetry, or history-poetry, is never to allow hatred of a data-target, or the heat of a case, to arouse one, or to wire one up, to the point of insanity, or violence, or to the condoning of racism, or killing. Treason against gentleness.

D.

It is therefore my belief that virtually every major poet's work in France and America for the past 100 years has prepared the civilization for the rebirth of history poesy. The *Wasteland, The Bridge, The Cantos,* W. C. Williams' *Paterson, The Maximus Poems,* Ginsberg's *Ankor Wat, Howl* and *Wichita Vortex Sutra,* the work of Snyder, in, say,

Turtle Island, and Jerome Rothenberg in *Poland 1931,* all
betoken an era of investigative poesy, a form of historical
writing—this is as potentially dangerous to the poet as a
minefield or those small foot-snuffing blow-up devices the
defense dept. used in Vietnam; but it is a danger thrill-
somely magnetic to a bard wandering through the electro-
magnetic aeon.

History-poesy, or investigative poetry, can thrive in our
era because of the implications of a certain poetic insight,
that is, in the implications of the line, "Now is the time for
prophecy without death as a consequence," from *Death to
Van Gogh's Ear,* a Ginsberg poem from 1958.

Investigative poesy is freed from capitalism, churchism,
and other totalitarianisms; free from racisms, free from alle-
giance to napalm-dropping military police states—a poetry
adequate to discharge from its verse-grids the undefiled high
energy purely-distilled verse-frags, using *every* bardic skill
and meter and method of the last 5 or 6 generations, in order to describe *every* aspect (no more secret governments!)
of the historical present, while aiding the future, even
placing bard-babble once again into a role as shaper of the
future.

For this is the era of the description of *the All;* the age
wherein a Socrates would have told the judges to take a
walk down vomit alley, and could have lived as an active ve-
hement leader of the Diogenes Liberation Squadron of
Strolling Troubadors and Muckrakers, till the microbes
'whelmed him. The era of police-statists punishing citizens
for secret proclivities is over. Blackmail, in other words, is
going to go bye-bye. One will not in any way have to assure
one's readers (to quote, is it Martial, or Catullus?) that
"pagina lasciva, vita proba," but rather it is now most definitely the age of *"pagina lasciva, vita lascivior."* And we are
here speaking of uncompunctious conjugation, not of riches
cutting up cattle from silent helicopters, or of bankers whipping each other on yachts.

Thrills course upward from the typewriter keys as my fingers type the words that say that poets are free from the nets

of any *particular* verse-form or verse-mind. Keats would have grown old in such a freedom. The days of bards chanting dactylic hexameters while strumming the phormingx, or lyre, trying to please some drooly-lipped war-lord are over, o triumphant beatnik spores! It's over! And the days of bards trying to please some CIA-worshipping cold war tough-liberal professor are done! done! done!

But the way of Historical Poesy, as I said earlier, is mined with danger, especially to those bards who would seek to drag the corpses of J.P. Morgan's neo-confederates through the amphetamine piranha tank.

For let us not forget for one microsecond that the government throughout history has tried to suppress, stomp down, hinder, or buy off dissident or left-wing poets.[1]

One has only to recall that Coleridge and Wordsworth one day were lounging by the sea shore, while nearby sat an English police agent on snitch patrol prepared to rush to headquarters to quill a report about the conversation.[2]

Or one can read that remarkable book, *William Blake and the Age of Revolution* by J. Bronowski, which Harper & Row printed in 1965, to see how reactionary English creeps, with their threats of jail, or worse, for accurately depicting the nature of the early parts of the French Revolution—how these reactionary creeps caused, in a significant way, poets like William Blake, who after all was a friend of Thomas Paine, to back away from historical poetry, and to retreat, if that is the word, into a poetry of symbols, where people like King George and William Pitt and others were known by code names such as Palamabron and Rintrah.[3]

Nor let us forget that the federal government tried to seize the first printing of *Howl and Other Poems* (it was printed abroad by City Lights) as it was coming into San Francisco bay.

Nor shall we forget the repressive corona of puke-vectors that I believe drove Shelley—censored, hounded by police statists, fearful of arrest—to take upon himself a self-destruction (rest in peace, o d.a. levy) and to set sail into a mad air; nor forget ever the corona of puke-vectors that sent the empty carriages of the rich shuttling along behind the cortege bearing the body of Byron.[4]

Nor shall we forget the fate of Ovid, who because that calmed-down murderer, Augustus, didn't like his book and the implications of his book *Ars Amatoria,* was sent away from the literary scene to die in exile.[5]

Nor shall we forget that Dostoevsky was standing ready to die in front of the firing squad when the reprieve arrived enabling him later on to "objectify" his stance into that of a jealous rightwing nut.[6]

Nor shall we forget how the Chilean poet-singer Victor Jara was leading a group of singers while imprisoned in the soccer stadium following the 1973 CIA-coup in Chile, and the killers chopped off his fingers to silence his guitar, and still he lead the singing—til they killed him, another bard butchered because of the U.S. secret police.

Nor shall we forget how the Czar's secret police hounded Alexandr Pushkin with a nightmare of surveillance and exile. In fact, a brief look at certain aspects of Pushkin's life is here appropriate, in order to guage some of the pressures that can force a poet "to become more objective," or, as the English professor who writes for a CIA-funded magazine might giggle, "to come to terms with the harsh facts of life." Or to escape into the forgetful symbols.

Notes

1. *The* Secret Police Sell-out Rule: *time after time as we read the biographies of writers, our hearts are broken as we monitor a hideous drift, passing, say, the 33rd year, to the cautious right. Sometimes I think that the secret police of the world developed a procedure at least 300 years ago to deal with the potential of the brilliant young to create quick change. And the* Secret Police Sell-out Rule *would go something like this: "If you can stomp them and punish them enough in their youth and middle age, then they'll calm down, the punks, and silently assent to the Corrupting It." Energy bio-dwindle also adds to the sell-out rule. And, if I go to prison, what will happen to my 15,000 books?*

2. *Someone should write well the story of Citizen Threlwell. If we all do not have the free chance to enact our own Threlwellean maneuvers, then we are still slaves. The point is that a visit by Threlwell was enough to cause you (Wordsworth) to lose your house and for the fuzz to slap a surveillance on you.*

3. *We are not here saying that Blake's* The French Revolution *is the world's greatest poem. And obviously Rintrah is a much more groovy name than Henry Kissinger (one way to deal with baleful names such as Kissinger's, in poems, would be, as the language gets more "glyphic" again, to conceive of a cacoglyph—a drawing or symbol (cacoglyph being the opposite of the sacred-or-hieroglyph) depicting, say, Kissinger. But we must, on the other hand, be wary of polishing such specks of evil til they become our shiniest art, if you can scan my zone.*

John Clarke, certainly one of the finest scholars of Blake, responded to the manuscript of Investigative Poetry with a poem, which speaks right to the essence of the Blake problem:

AS TO THE DISSIMULATION

It is true certainly Blake suffered from Nervous Fear & because of it retreated into a poetry of symbols, but, ironically, this retreat was truer to his Good Angel than had he quickly & easily, like Oedipus solved, being a Mental Prince, the case of history under investigation, for, lo & behold, he found something deeper behind, going on, States which only Individuals were in, not fused with Eternally, but retrievable, a true cosmological narrative to be written as distinct from its Generated denominations, whose accomplishment is only what allows us today to be political, his system gave us the tools of our profession.

Sept 17, 1975

Yes. And Blake's stance is Absolute Integrity, *without which Investigative Poetry is immoral gibberish—and his drive toward the hieratic poem-glyph is ever our investigative grail.*

And I have no quarrel with Blake's vision of a whole system of Self—a Self that paints, designs and sings the limnations of God or Godot or Gododd. What I quarrel with is the with-

*drawal from the polis—and into the polis thus neglected will
march totalitarian apostles: nixon, hitler, stalin, haldeman,
helms—abetted by the kings and queens of satan (the lovers of
violence).*

About 1789
William Blake moved to small house
on south side of Thames

got cooking there
on Prophetic Books

decided through visits and advice of the
received ghost of his brother Robert

to design in reverse relief on etched
copper plates, both poem and design—

and then to adorn the printed-
poem with individual paintings

thank you, o ghost.

Hand-held press
Hand-etched copper plates
Hand-pigmented poem-glyphs

The hand! The hand!

And as he fashioned and painted more and more of his books

He moved
Toward
Soul-Scroll.

And Blake's techniques in preparing and producing say, The
Songs of Innocence and Experience, *the move toward poem-
glyph, should ever be an archetype for the Investigative Poet.
Print it yrself, adorn it yrself, send it out yrself, and make it
sacred.*
    *4. Shelley and government spy-scum: "at last he gave up, sent
forward a box filled with his books, which was inspected by the
government and reported as seditious, and on April 4 left Ire-*

land (1812). He settled ten days later at Nantgwilt, near Cwm
Elan, the seat of his cousins, the Groves, and there remained un-
til June. In this period he appears to have met Peacock, through
whom he was probably introduced to his London Publisher,
Hookham. In June he again migrated to Lynmouth in Devon.
Here he wrote, his 'Letter to Lord Ellenborough,' defending
Eaton, who had been sentenced for publishing Paine's Age of
Reason *in a periodical. He amused himself by putting copies of*
the Declaration of Rights, *(Shelley's revolutionary pamphlet*
from French sources) and a new satirical poem, The Devil's
Walk, *in bottles and fire balloons, and setting them adrift by sea*
and air; but a more mundane attempt to circulate the Declaration of Rights *resulted unfortunately for his servant (I guess*
we have to forgive Shelley for having servants), who had become
attached to him and followed him from Ireland, and was
punished by a fine of 200 pounds or eight month's imprison-
ment for posting it on the walls of Barnstable. Shelley could not
pay the fine, but he provided fifteen shillings a week to make
the prisoner's confinement more comfortable. The government
now put Shelley under surveillance, and he was watched by
Leeson, a spy. . . . *and it is known that Shelley was dogged*
by Leeson, whom he feared long afterwards."

> *from the biographical sketch in*
> Complete Poetical Works *of*
> *Percy Bysshe Shelley*
> *Cambridge Edition, 1901*

There is nothing like having a hateful person, paid by
a government agency, company or private party, enter
your life spewing nodules of mix-up, dissension, hate,
violence, fear.

(take a quick check into the specifics for instance,
of the FBI cointelpro fear-and-death ruinations.)

5. *Every time I get out my 11th edition of the* Encyclopaedia
Britannica *(vol. 20, ODE to PAY), I suffer the frothing anger-*
electrics reading about the injustices suffered by Ovid, driven to
the Black Sea by a punk turkey tyrant snuffer. And it could well

*happen again—the androids with book-burning lasers to knock
at a poet's door with a computerized printout of the plot of her
latest poem.*

   *6. One can understand how Dostoevsky drifted to the right,
being a heavy Russian nationalist at heart—but o lord how
could he have ever accepted inside himself, first that he deserved
a sentence of death, or deserved a commutation that gave him 5
hideous years in the slams, and for what? For conspiring to print
copies of Belinsky's revolutionary letter of response to the late
life god-grovels of Gogol.*

Alexandr Pushkin

d.o.b. 5-26-1799
d. 1-29-1837
shot in stomach

       friends
    with pre-Decembrists
       secret societies, but never trusted with
plot-plans. They never trust poets.
    belonged to Green Lamp which may have
been a branch of the Union of Welfare, freethinking
    orgiasts and partisans of Liberty.
Pushkin's cry of "Tremble, o tyrants of the world
    And you . . . o fallen slaves, arise!"
    (Ode to Freedom, 1817)

may not have been so loudly heard in the casinos of
Petrograd but it is said that the revolutionary poems of
his youth were so sung in the mind that the soldiers in the
barracks knew them by heart

    —9 of 10, it is said, of the young in Russia then re-
ceived their revolutionary input from Pushkin

    His political poems, like the secret Russian tracts of to-
day, were passed from hand to hand in manuscript.

The fuzz were hip to the trip, and harassed Pushkin. In 1820, he nearly was bricked into prison, so chose a period of exile in the south.

During these years of police surveillance, Pushkin gradually began to soften under the pressure, becoming "more objective"—that is, secreting his revolutionary politics in narrative.

6 years of police harassment, til Sept of 1826, the new Czar, Nicolas I, summoned him to Moscow, and announced that he, the Czar, henceforth would be the poet's "censor." And although the poet's formal exile was over, the chief of the Russian Secret Police kept him under the shackles of surveillance. Pushkin had to submit all his writings to the Czar for approval.

In March of 1826, he was to write in a letter, "I do not intend foolishly to oppose the generally accepted order." (As, and probably under similar fearful pressure, William Blake in 1791 had decided not to print *The French Revolution*.)

Three years
Pushkin in Moscow and Petrograd, a dissipated period of surveillance, drinking, gambling, fucking—wrote very little—a right-winger's vision of paradise for a poet.
1927/8/9
And in the 1830's Pushkin studied in the Russian State Archives going back to the texts and documents.
Pressure
      force the poets
              pressure
                   to weaken
                        pressure
                            the force
    of their beliefs.
    Never Again.

    At the great religious
    festivals of antiquity
    the poets sang/chanted
    for prizes—

and in the era of the Investigative Poet
the Diogenes Troubador Data Squads
will chew their way into the
gory dressing room of Richard Helms

But what is the prize?
The prize is for the poets
to assume their rightful
positions as chroniclers
of the Time Track,
of the historical moment
whether century, aeon, hour
or microsecond

As Olson said: "I would be an historian as Herodotus Was,
looking for oneself for the evidence of what is said."

But what is the prize?
the prize is for Diogenes Eleutherarchs
waving the banner of
enforced economic equality
to weaken, to lessen,
and to bring down into the vale of Ha Ha Hee
the North American CIA Police State,

and for poets
never again
to internalize grovelness.

Photo by Alan Rabold

Allen Ginsberg

VISIONS OF ORDINARY MIND: (1948-1955): DISCOURSE W/ QUESTIONS & ANSWERS

JUNE 9, 1976

Edited by Paul Portugés & Allen Ginsberg

ALLEN GINSBERG: My father wrote what was called in the twenties "lyric poetry," and I got my ear from him to begin with. Some major exponents of that kind of poetry were Eleanor Wylie, Edna St. Vincent Millay and Edward Arlington Robinson. A.E. Housman was a big influence then in the standard anthology used by poets that belonged to the Poetry Society of America, an organization in New York that had kicked out Maxwell Bodenhein after he pissed on the floor at a public meeting in 1927 (or something like that). The Poetry Society of America had a standard notion of style. At its best, it was the Edward Arlington Robinson genre, *Miniver Cheevy,* or *Eros Tyrannos,* great poem:

> Meanwhile we do no harm, for they
> That with a god have striven
> Not caring much for what we say
> Take what the god has given,
> Though like waves breaking it may be
> Or like a changed familiar tree
> Or like a stairway to the sea
> Where down the blind are driven.

That series of linked stanzas has a very powerful clanging rhyme.

Louis Untermeyer was, I guess, the anthology king and taste maker (as Oscar Williams' *Little Treasury* was the standard anthology circulated in colleges in the fifties, and Don Allen's *New American Poetry* set other standards post-sixties), and Untermeyer's taste was for his own style of poetry, lyric, similar to my father's, like his *Caliban in the Coal Mine,* a very simple rhymed statement. I picked up on the iambic rhyme, stressed verse, I was brought up on it. For my high school graduation book, I wrote a sonnet which I've forgotten by now, but which went something like, "We face the glorious future, da da dee and we're off into our pomp maturity." Just a goofy high school sonnet, valedictorian's pentameter. So all the poems I wrote when I was sixteen or eighteen were sleepwalking repetitions of sounds I'd heard in Robinson or Edna Millay. And their sounds were like sleepwalking repetitions of sounds they had read in Wyatt and Surrey or Shakespeare. The whole form has degenerated, yet it was still called "lyric poetry." Originally "lyric" because it was done with strings, with a lyre, those forms were songs at one time. Then people stopped singing poems in these forms for the general public, until Dylan, probably, as far as most poets were involved. Yeats wrote lyric poetry, but he always had "a chune in his head," but he was one of the very few people who did.

So by the time I was twenty-two, I was still writing that same kind of verse except that all of a sudden I had a funny kind of visionary experience (or a "psychedelic experience") which completely changed my attitude toward poetry. I was examining Blake's pages and heard Blake's voice in a sort of interesting hallucination, without any drugs, in 1948. So I realized after that it was possible in a poem to reproduce some body rhythm which if inserted in other peoples' bodies might catalyze a similar experience, 'cause that's what happened to me.[1]

PAUL PORTUGÉS: Were there some specific Blake poems that caused your visionary episode?

A.G.: The particular poems that turned me on in Blake were *The Sunflower* and *The Sick Rose* and a couple others. [*He sings Blake's* The Sick Rose.]

P.P.: Did your experience have much effect on your own poetry?

A.G.: Having had a visionary experience out of these little poems, Blake's, my initial reaction to getting turned on, mentally, poetically, spiritually, was to create little mysterious verses similar: "Many seek and never see, / anyone can tell them why . . ." (From *The Eye Altering Alters All.*[2]) I thought I was making a sort of mystical riddle as to the nature of consciousness, but actually, the whole—there's no content in it. It's just sort of like a paranoic reference. Like going around staring at people's eyes saying "Many seek and never see," but I thought that's what poetry was supposed to do. Sort of penetrate the skull by some eye stare or some hypnotic rhythm. "I cannot sleep, I cannot sleep / until a victim is resigned; / a shadow holds me in his keep / and seeks the bones that he must find."[3] The same kind of rhyme like "Though like waves breaking it may be / Or like a changed familiar tree, / Or like a stairway to the sea / Where down the blind are driven."[4] An echo of that insistent, prophetic, very abstract sound with no specific imagery, no automobiles, no fingernails, no noses. I thought of poetry then as hermetic, containing some kind of mystical secret of consciousness, which would be referred to by symbols. If you talked about "bones," if you talked about "light," that would turn people on to the area of consciousness you were talking about; it might even catalyze that consciousness in them. By "that consciousness" I mean some kind of big open mystical consciousness, like on acid. (I hadn't had acid at the time.)

P.P.: Did you hear Blake's voice reading or singing his poems?

A.G.: Yeah, I had my eye on the page, and I heard a big solid, solemn earthen voice saying Ah, Sunflower, weary of time . . . My voice *now*, actually! I had a much higher voice then. What I heard was my own voice now, or say

about five or ten or so years ago, when I was in stronger
voice—the peak of health. By hindsight, I've always been
mystified by that experience; I've never really figured it out.
It was actually an auditory hallucination, I heard a voice,
and went around for weeks and months and years telling
people I heard Blake's voice. "I heard Blake's voice!" Like
an acid head who's had some transcendental vision and goes
around trying to beat you over the head with it and insist-
ing that it come true right now! Like everybody take their
clothes off right now, or like revolution now! Or like what—
electricity now! CIA now! Breakthrough now! You know
that syndrome.

P.P.: Can you explain it some more?

A.G.: It's a realization that there is one common
consciousness, and that if only everybody would refer to that
consciousness simultaneously there would be some universal
cosmic consciousness breakthrough—so that everybody at the
same time would be the same sublime self. And would be
telepathizing the same perceptions back and forth!

P.P.: Was your vision a classical visionary experience, like
St. John of the Cross? You know, hearing voices, having a
feeling of light . . .

A.G.: Well, yeah . . . but what do, what are classical
visionary experiences like?

P.P.: Like in St. Teresa, or in other famous visionary accounts—they all heard voices, like you mentioned with
Blake, and there were sensations of light . . .

A.G.: Okay, as far as light—I had a sensation of that everyday light as becoming some kind of eternal light. So it was
like an eternal light superimposed on everyday light, but everyday light wasn't any different than everyday light! It was
just, "the eye altering alters all."[5] My eyes, having altered,
everyday light seemed like sunlight in eternity. So there was
a sensation of awe, spaciousness and ancientness as in some
eternity, but actually people get that everyday. I mean,
aren't we now in eternity?—by "now" this is years later—I
don't know what was so striking about it . . . but it
seemed to me like a complete break in nature, or a break in

the normal continuum of my consciousness. In classical religious experience, like in James' *Varieties of Religious Experiences*, there's a reference to light, as if it's something special. And there *is* a sensation of something special! Like in acid, when you go out in the day, and you're not hallucinating, you're just seeing the normal air and light of the day. You can't say it's any different than everyday light, can you—really?

P.P. Well, the acid, the acid . . .

A.G.: It may seem different, but basically the big discovery is that everyday light is supernatural! Does that make sense? Is there anybody that disagrees with that? So if everyday light seems supernatural—thus the line of Blake's—"the eye altering alters all." So, change your brain, change your eyeballs, and the light seems awesome. So what are the characteristics of the light? It seems like it's eternal, in the sense that it's always been there, timeless, translucent, you can see through it . . .

P.P.: Like the later afternoon light through the leaves of trees . . . Bright . . .

A.G.: Gracious, because it allows you to see. So there's a certain kind of intelligence in the light because it's built to allow you to see. It seems like some intentionality to the light. It's cooperating with your consciousness, 'cause without the light you wouldn't be able to . . . whatever it is . . . words . . . but . . . the particular experience I had without drugs. I was taken completely by surprise; I was overtaken because I hadn't expected anything like that.

P.P.: Do you ever think of having prepared yourself, in some unconscious or conscious way for the visions?

A.G.: I hadn't been seeing friends, I had a sort of social breakdown. Burroughs was away, and Kerouac was away, I'd graduated from school, so I was at the end of my youthful rope. I was living alone in East Harlem and eating mostly vegetables. I had kind of gotten into a nervous breakdown, given up on my life, and just didn't know what or where I was, I was living alone, so there was an absence of preoccupation, absence of plans, a dead end. I had come to a

dead end, like most kids do when they get out of college, got
to make it in the world, get a job, they don't know what to
do, don't want to confront the anxiety of unemployment office, "getting your shit together," suit of clothes, reality becoming real, I was in a kind of limbo period where I had no
security, no assurance of what I was headed for. An open future. The only special thing on that specific occasion was
that I had just jacked off. I don't know if you've ever done
that, but jacking off while reading . . . sort of an absent-
minded jacking off. Sort of special kind of pleasure,
masturbatory pleasure, being distracted in the mind, and
the body having its own life.

p.p.: Do you think the rhythms or rhymes of the poems
you were reading affected your state of mind?

a.g.: Well, the particular poetry I was reading was Blake's,
which has rhyme . . . [He reads and sings Blake's Ah!
Sunflower.]

question: This modern poetry, uh, it doesn't have to
rhyme, is that right?

a.g.: Modern poetry? We'll be talking about that later,
right now I'm just talking about old-fashioned rhymed
poetry, for which Blake was exemplary; and some rhymed,
old-fashioned-style poetry that I used to write when I was
eighteen to twenty-five.

p.p.: Had you been reading a lot of mystical literature
prior to your Blake visions?

a.g.: Yeah, I was going to say, St. John of the Cross, I was
reading a little bit of Plato's Phaedrus, and some Plotinus, a
little Luther—I had a lot of theology literature at hand set
up in egg-crate bookshelves by a student whose apartment
I'd sublet. And St. Teresa of Avila, Blake, a little Marvell.

Let's get back to the quality of that kind of breakthrough
experience—Has anybody here in class had visionary experience, what they thought was visionary experiences, outside
of drugs? Really raise hands so we get some clear signal—
[Majority raise hands.] Outside of drugs?! Well then OK.
How many people don't feel they've had any visionary experience outside of the drug scene? [Scattering of hands.]

How many people have had some sort of visionary experience *with* drugs? [*Majority raise hands.*] How many have
had *no* visionary experience of any kind? [*Few hands
raised.*] Raise your hands! [*Still few hands raised.*] That's
terrific! OK. These are probably the saints here . . . so
(nearly) everybody's had some light—It's amazing. I didn't
realize that it was so common for people to have
had . . .

Q: But the quality of the vision may be different . . . ?

A.G.: I don't think so, probably I'm more loud-mouthed
about it.

Q: How did you feel after visions? What were your first
reactions?

A.G.: "Many seek and never see / anyone can tell them
why / . . . I ask many, they ask me / This is a great mystery."
. . . A slightly paranoid element's there because I was
thinking all the time: Everybody's going around really
secretly asking everybody else: have you seen *the light*?
Have you seen it? That's why "I ask many, they ask me, /
This is a great mystery." I had the idea that all conversation
even about the butcher shop, secretly referred to the infinite
light of the mystical experience.

P.P.: And you changed your mind?

A.G.: Well, I . . . yes. Sure, why not. Yeah, I'll get to
that later. My immediate thought was "Many seek and
never see." Meaning: many people have the idea of looking
for a God, truth, looking for beauty, but actually never at-
tain some breakthrough of consciousness, into a totally fresh
eternal awesome-world visionary experience. However, everybody does experience it, whether they know it or not,
but, most of the people push it to the back of their mind.
Or've had some glimpse, but put it in the back of their
mind and don't bank on it, or don't count it as social
currency, don't talk about it. For that reason: "Anyone can
tell them why."[6] "Anyone" is practically the majority of this
class, the majority of this class could tell them why. "And
never take until they try." I thought that perhaps there was
some element—you could catalyze it, if you were willful, or

if you really threw yourself into the search for vision, you
could bring it about. "Unless they try it in their
sleep"—How many people had visionary experiences in
dreams? [*Muddled speech from class.*] Has anybody not?
. . . You haven't had it in your sleep? You can't remember. First thing in the morning check back. So: "And never
take until they try / Unless they try it in their sleep / And
never some until they die." That's because I'd assumed that
death was complete consciousness. There's a line in T.S.
Eliot: "The complete fire is death." I thought he meant that
when you die, everything opens up, and you see ALL! So: "I
ask many, they ask me, / This is a great mystery." I titled it,
The Eye Altering Alters All, out of Blake, a direct reference
to a visionary experience: actually, it was the first poem I
wrote immediately after that Blake audition.

P.P.: Can you spend some time describing the visions
. . . after almost thirty years, do you remember what
happened?

A.G.: What happened to me was: one afternoon in Harlem,
I had been reading the Blake poems. Heard, as I say an "audition," of a very deep voice reciting three or four poems—
first *The Sunflower*, then *The Sick Rose*, and then *The
Little Girl Lost*. I wasn't quite sure about the time span involved—there was the sound of a voice in the room that
didn't seem to be coming from inside my head. Seemed to
be a voice in the room. But nobody was there. Recognizably
Blake, simply from The Ancient of Days feeling about it. I
thought it was the Creator, God, I associated it with a God
some anciency, prophetic. At the same time, there was outside the window a sense of extraordinarily clear light. The
everyday afternoon sunlight but with extraordinary clarity
as if the light itself were some sort of bright intelligent substance, revealing all of the intelligent handiwork of the Ancient of Days, the working of ancient days. And the first
thing I noticed outside the window were the cornices of the
buildings in Harlem—1880's, 1890's, 1910 apartments. In
those days there was quite a bit of handiwork, hand work.
Like stone chiseled—

Q: Friezes?

A.G.: On apartment houses . . . friezes . . . the special metal artwork for the roof, overhangs, done in slight Greek or Roman style. Little cornucopias, or cornices, or scroll-work—I don't know architectural terms. Do you know what I'm talking about? Well, it was the first time I looked at the roofcombs of those old-fashioned tenement apartments—very carefully, and they were silhouetted against the bright living light of the sky, which sky-light seemed endless in blue. Standing up like buttresses in eternity! Somewhat as in the Magic Squares, paintings of Paul Klee when seen optic in 3-D. Giant foundations and buttresses were the cornices of the buildings and I suddenly realized that an enormous amount of conscious intelligence had gone into their creation. A great deal of care, a great deal of planning, a great deal of love, in the sense that people put their bodies to work, six flights up in the air creating these sculptures, which nobody ever noticed, in the street, generations, nobody noticed them, or I had never paid any attention to them. And I suddenly saw them as signs calling for my attention. They were signaling to me from 1890, intelligible comments. Anonymous, thousands and thousands of invisible workmen all over New York in 1890 had made intelligible comments throughout the building tops of the city. Street after street there was all this sublime cosmic intelligence, made out of metal.

P.P.: Intelligence, what do you mean?

A.G.: Intelligence in the sense that—of writing for the eyes. Signals that they were there. Workmen were there and they were quite conscious in 1890, and had built something in eternity for me to look at fifty or sixty years later. It'd never occurred to me that people were full of wisdom, or that there was that much transmission of consciousness in material forms throughout the civilized world. And then I looked further, say, at the clouds that were passing over, and they too seemed created by some hand to be conscious signals also—just like the cornices. Signals of some kind of intelligence. An intelligence much vaster more far-reaching

than a workman's hand because there's the Whatever ac-
cumulation of energy and force and suffering and
consciousness that would have taken for animals to die and
their blood to dry and be evaporated and brought up into
the skies and the oceans to be drawn up into the skies and
formed into clouds and then drift over New York and drop
rain. See, that enormous amount of work had gone into
making clouds. Millions and billions of years of work to
make the entire structure I was sitting in the middle of, an
entire planetary solar system! And then all of a sudden, I
looked up beyond the cornices into the sky, and the sky
seemed to be a creation of a great Ancientness and a much
vaster creation than anything I had thought of as Poetry. So
I had the impression of the entire universe as poetry filled
with light and intelligence and communication and signals.
Kind of like the top of my head coming off, letting in the
rest of the universe connected into my own brain.

   Q: Can you get any sense of expansion by retelling by re-
calling that experience now?

   A.G.: At the moment, yes, because it seems so obvious.
While talking, I've been looking out and seeing very bright
greenery, bright golden light outside the green door and
trees swaying in a very gentle muscular wind. If I look for it
I can . . . Well, I don't want to get into analysis yet, I'm
still trying to get to the Suchness . . . some poetic description. By hindsight, I think that I was, in adolescence, so
limited in my view that what I discovered was ordinary
consciousness! What I was discovering was mere ordinary everyday consciousness, or ordinary mind, so to speak. The sky
is big, the light is bright! It's just that I'd never noticed it,
never appreciated it. In other words, what I took to be supernatural vision was just natural growing up, I was just becoming conscious, waking up to what was ordinary. By this
time I'm so used to it that it now seems ordinary, it doesn't
seem supernatural at all: maybe then just waking up to
what I thought was supernatural, which everybody else had
been seeing all along. It's just that I was the only one in the
universe that never noticed that, see. So that's why I made

such a big deal out of it. It was my nightmare, that I was the only one that had never noticed the sky. I had been so limited and dumb that what I was discovering was what everybody knew already, and I was *afraid* that that was the truth. And probably that was the truth, for nowadays I've come to decide maybe it's best that I alone was Blindman, because thus everybody's already living in Eternity and I don't have to worry about it anymore. Rather than claiming it as my exclusive territory . . . I've never really talked about this in a class before, interesting, kind of mind-blowing see, because I asked how many here had visions? and two-thirds *have* had, actually I'm curious, what have other people gone through?

Q: . . . The reason people don't talk about these . . . because it tends to dilute the experience . . . Although talk also realizes the experience . . . or else talk about it you lose the experience. . . . Also there's the pain of being separated from that experience . . .

P.P.: Didn't your experience, state of heightened consciousness, last over a period of a week or two? . . . It wasn't just a day?

A.G.: No, it was intermittent. It actually was quite limited. The first day, there were three separate occasions, and I can't measure the time, I've been baffled by that. Because it might have been just a second, but it seemed like a long bath of time, twenty minutes, half an hour. And as I became conscious of experiencing it, it closed down, and my ordinary consciousness returned.

P.P.: What do you mean?

A.G.: See, as I was sitting there in a sort of state of suspended mind and suspended awe, no, suspended decision, suspended mental activity—then when I said, "Oh, I'm Allen Ginsberg, I'm having this particular visionary experience, isn't that great? I'm a poet, I'll be able to use this for the rest of my life," then all of a sudden. . . . "Oh, let me see, what was I having, what is going on!" . . . It was very paradoxical and immediately you become self-conscious, immediately you think, your Eye closes down. Very similar to meditation experience, too . . . later.

Q: Isn't there a conscious cultivation of these experiences now, that's why everyone raised their hands . . . Everybody body has visions but not everybody knows it?

A.G.: "Many seek and never see, / Anyone can tell them why." My theory then was that everybody knew all along, and everybody was in a sense in a permanent state of heightened consciousness. Or that there were several consciousnesses going on at once. Which you can say is true: when you recall yourself, when you do enter a state of remembrance, you realize that you remembered all along. That's one of the tearful and great things about mind, you realize that you've known all along. Maybe on the death bed or drowning there's that awareness: "Ah, all along I've been aware of this, it's just that I didn't pay attention to what I knew most deeply, and basically, "Yes, yes, / that's what / I wanted, / I always wanted, / I always wanted, / to return / to the body / where I was born."[7a]

P.P.: Back in 1948, people would think you were crazy if you told them how sublime, how visionary they were or could be.

A.G.: Oh, yeah. There's an acknowledgement in our culture now of those areas of experience as being real. At the time, 1948, when it happened to me, it wasn't anything that people discussed and it was not part of the background of the culture. There's an extraordinary difference between the consciousness of consciousness of the seventies and the consciousness of consciousness of the forties. One didn't— there was no real examination of the nature of consciousness, or the suchness of consciousness or the varieties of consciousness, or alterations of mind. They didn't have the terminology like "alternative mode of consciousness," "modalities of consciousness." They didn't have the terminology to discuss it: or they had a mystical terminology, like "I saw light." So I rushed into Columbia College's English office, Mark Van Doren's, saying "I just saw the light!" The only one who asked me what I meant, was Mark Van Doren.

The others just thought I was just a nut, you know, a typical college kid who'd freaked out finally, not gone out and got a job, instead freaked out. I thought, "They're right, I'd better get a job."

CYRUS [*Aet. 72*]: People back in those times were afraid. They were afraid. They thought they were going crazy or . . .

A.G.: Precisely . . . do you remember that? Talking now about the forties.

CYRUS: The forties sure. Thirties.

A.G.: Did you have any special experience in those days?

CYRUS: Yes, I? I went crazy sometimes.

A.G.: Any kind of illumination feeling?"

CYRUS: Illumination, that you're talking about, didn't come till later, here . . . the seventies.

A.G.: His Bodhisattva name is Patience.

CYRUS: Where'd you find that out?

A.G.: We took vows together.

CYRUS: Oh yes, so we did.

A.G.: . . . I'm knocked out, just trying to figure what's the actual common ground between us here, in the room. . . . I'd been talking Solitary, as if vision were just my own property. But obviously now everybody owns a piece of that property.

Q.: Anglo-Saxons had language for it . . .

A.G.: McClure has descriptions, borrowed from Anglo-Saxon, Aelf-land and Aelf-sheen, a sort of hermetic language referring to magical experience, also good practical nature mind description—Aelf-skin, a glow, "there are Halos around each being . . . the aura of the past that is beauty." His terminology lately is Beauty, just simple, and his detail's minute, like nature . . .

P.P.: It's hard to make others understand a phenomena strange as Visions.

A.G.: It's most interesting if you can see something visionary about this room, for example, and point it out to other people so they can get a vision. Rather than see something visionary somewhere else that nobody can see, and you can

only describe it to the corridor of nurds! But you can actually point to the peculiar flicker of light of the electric
machine hanging from the ceiling—make people see it so
they suddenly realize a flourescent tube as a kind of Raw
Intelligence beast hanging from the ceiling—that was my raw
intention, then, anyway.

P.P.: Are you, or were you sure that everyone had the ability to see in a new way?

A.G.: Are we all seeing, having the same vision? Or are we
all having different visions in different universes out of different brains and different eyeballs and are they all discon-
tinuous? That's one thing I don't know either, it's something
to discuss in public, and somewhat clarify. My original idea
was that what I was seeing was what everybody must see,
or will come to see, or has seen, since "Egypt" on. "Go
back to Egypt and the Greeks . . ." [*He reads* A Mad
Gleam.[7]] That was one of those early poems, trying to *refer*
to the vision. But it was still "reference" to the vision, rather
than "presentation" of detail. (Ezra Pound's terminology.)
So I concluded, finally, that only presentation of detail—
what you *saw*—speaks and transmits to other people the mental quality of visionary realization. You can't communicate
accurately by conglomerating abstractions. Poetry's power is
that you can remember, and then write down little details
. . . sometimes even while you are seeing. I always specu-
lated that William Carlos Williams, a modern common-
sense naturalist poet, was really recording a high moment of
perception, Vision, when he said: "So much depends on a
red wheelbarrow glazed with rain water beside the white
chickens." As if he made a little symbolic icon of a moment
of heightened consciousness. Probably he was just saying to
himself, let's see what kind of detail I can write down. Now
I doubt that he was, in fact, making a representation of a
special moment of *my* kind of visionary experience detail.

P.P.: Did Williams see any of his poems in terms of visions
or illumination?

A.G.: I never asked him . . . it may be that this "Vision"
is just ordinary consciousness and people are so daydreamy

and neurotic that they're just not in their bodies, not seeing what's in front of them most of the time anyway. So Williams was experiencing it as *ordinary* everyday Rutherford consciousness, while I, for long decades' time, thought it was special heightened consciousness, even visionary.

P.P.: Did you relate your visionary experience to that Blakean concept of "eternity in a grain of sand," the eternal in the ordinary?

A.G.: You find eternity in the roof-cornice of a Harlem apartment. I see that that's what he meant, to see in any part any place in the universe some fragment of an infinitely vast design. Whether it be the red brick or seven-colored squares of wall-facing [*pointing to classroom wall*] which were assembled from many corners of Colorado, or God knows where all the sand and water came from to plaster up on that wall, and where the hands came from that put it there. Like an assemblage of phantoms to get just that wall up, and the wall itself still here shining out. So that's part of a larger design, eternal, all the way back.

Q: Did you think you're the ultimate perceiver, or that there's an outside perceiver perceiving you, or you're someone else's hallucination?

A.G.: All those questions came up later. At that moment, however, my impression was that someone was perceiving me, and I was perceiving that someone had perceived me all along: that the Ancient of Days was perceiving me and had been perceiving me, and that I was just waking up and perceiving back.

P.P.: What . . . (???)

A.G.: There was a sense of an Eternal Father completely conscious caring about me in whom I had just wakened. I had just wakened into his brain, or into his consciousness, a larger consciousness than my own. Which was identical with my own consciousness but which was also the consciousness of the entire universe. So basically it was a sensation of the entire universe being completely conscious.

A little historical poetical footnote: there seemed to be a number of significant poetic visionary experiences in that

year, 1948. Gary Snyder reported similarly—in 1948 he'd finished a big essay—his mental-scholarship rational work, his
Reed College senior thesis—and then went down to the
banks of the Willamette River and sat down before sunrise
in total silence, exhausted, with this year's long intellectual
effort completed—finished all that night. And just as the sun
rose, in a complete dead silence and his own body exhausted, just as a crack of light appeared in the sky, thousands
and thousands of birds arose up out of the trees by the
river—birds which had been totally silent—he hadn't even
noticed they were there—filling the air with sentient
squawks. He suddenly realized that "everything was alive,"
that was his description, everything in the universe was
sentient, the entire universe was alive. It was '48 soon after
the bomb. I'd relate this historically, to some sort of large
scale planetary awakening of consciousness, some vaster
sentient consciousness, or less anthropocentric consciousness,
a more biocentric consciousness. As a result of the tolling of
the great iron gong of doom throughout the planet into any
consciousness that read the newspaper. Maybe the birds
didn't know, but all the humans knew that it was finally
possible to destroy consciousness too, or destroy brains all
over.

I started to try to trace the curve of my own development.
I remember "revolving around my own corpse," that is,
revolving around the corpse of the vision for many years.
The visions themselves came to an end abruptly within a
week or so, after several other episodes I won't describe—
with a final breakthrough or a final experience: I was walking around Columbia College campus at night, with one of
Blake's poems going around in my head, "O Rose, thou
art sick . . ." I had a distinct impression of that vast
conscious sky I'd glimpsed the week before; that it had now
turned on me and was going to eat me up—that this enormous power of consciousness that spread through the universe had taken a dislike to me, so to speak—or now that it
had noticed me—it was going to call me into it, devour me.
So that I, Allen, was going to disappear, absorbed into this

giant octopus serpent-monster consciousness. I think that's a
pretty common bad acid trip, probably it's a common visionary experience too. I mean it's completely real, that you realize that you the individual self eyeball is *going to die* and
be absorbed into a much larger intelligence. I had a kind of
shuddery experience, bad trip so to speak, which turned me
off. I thought I was somewhat in control of my consciousness
and could invoke a "breakthrough" at will, for about a
week, but the last time I tried invoking it, what I got was
the horrors, and I got frightened, and thought, uh oh, I've
gone crazy, I'd better not play with this anymore. Or I'd better find out something reliable about this breakthrough. Unfortunately, I didn't have any Tibetan lamas, Swamis,
gnostic esoteric poets, or rock musicians to turn to at that
point. There was nobody to talk to, that was the problem,
there was absolutely nobody to talk to who was, like, sane or
clear—more difficult than "coming out of the closet." The
few people I talked to told me to see a psychiatrist, or just
turned off, so I got very splenetic, angry and irritable, thinking that other people were resisting acknowledging what
they themselves knew. So it was a typical, visionary
misjudgment—you run across that kind of acid halluci-
nation-kid who insists that his vision be immediately understood and accepted—walk in front of automobiles naked,
revolution overnight, don't eat material food, etc.

Jump cut to London, 1973, Burroughs in St. James Street,
quote: "Anybody who makes an impression on you is a vampire," unquote. Dream that night: I was looking out of a
pub window in London—a mullioned window, with old, un-
clear-glass leaded squares. And I had an uncanny feeling
that some vampire was approaching down street; sure
enough, as I looked out the window, there was a long-haired
balding-top round-blue-faced figure, with black circles under
his eyes, fanged but human teeth, and a malevolent expression—and I recognized it was William Blake, come to
get me again. So I said, "Ah! at last, I'll go out and get that
bastard, check him out now. Vampire, eh? He'd been
feeding on my consciousness long enough." And when I

went out he got scared and ran away. That's the end of the dream.

I had come to the conclusion within ten minutes of the original 1948 visionary experiences, that any ratiocination or thinking about them would automatically interpose a screen and get between my own consciousness and open reality and fill it with thought, so I would be substituting memory of vision for vision. There's the vampire aspect. But I also had said—to myself at that same time—"Now that I've seen this heaven on earth, I will never forget it, I will never stop referring all things to it, I will never stop considering it the center of my human existence and the center of my life which is now changed into a new world, and I'll never be able to go back, and that's great; and from now on, I'm chosen, blessed, sacred, poet, and this is my sunflower, my new mind. I'll be faithful the rest of my life, and I'll never forget it, and never deny it, and I'll never renounce it." So finally, years later, I found I had to shit on it and renounce it to get the monkey off my back. I'm not speaking clearly enough . . .

P.P.: You mean trying to get back to it kept you away from it?

A.G.: As the visions faded, the actuality, there was nothing left but memory. I kept trying to go back in memory, to reconstitute the vision by staring at cornices or at trees or thinking that somehow I could recatalyze it. Take drugs to catalyze it, and acid does approximate that sensation of eternity. Well, on acid most of the time I also got the horror trip, because I was trying so hard to get back into the Eternity that I'd seen once before; so that every time I got high, when the first doubt came that I might not see "Eternity" . . . or the fear came that I might get eaten alive by "God," then the trip immediately turned into a hell. So my first thirteen psychedelic years were vomiting hells. And I didn't actually get out of that until I tried to combine acid with meditation. I got to India and saw Dudjom Rinpoche in 1963, and presented him with my psychological history, visionary history, my acid and peyote history, and he said very sympathetically that some images I described were similar to meditation experiences: "If you see anything horrible, don't cling to it; and if you see anything beautiful, don't cling to it." That formula actually cut the Gordian Knot of my mind there, because I realized that I *had* been clinging constantly to the memory of the vision. Because of my insistency, filling my head with thought about it, I cut myself off from direct perception—whether it was visionary or ordinary. In any case, I wasn't seeing what was in front of me—whether it be an eternity or just ordinary old Boulder. It's the same very simple situation you all know when you're young and trying to get laid, you think about it so much and make so many awkward efforts you don't get laid, whereas when you do relax you let things go their own way and do what comes naturally. Everybody knows that feedback of self-consciousness. So there's the old traditional statement, "Unless the seed die, it won't grow again." Or: "Only by renouncing, will you get what you want." Or what you thought you wanted. Death-in-life, the obvious order is to give up your idée fixe. Die, give up, let go, rather than force the issue.

P.P.: Are you talking about an experience of renouncing Blake visions on the train from Kyoto to Tokyo?

A.G.: That was a more superficial mental event. 1963, coming back from India, I realized that I wasn't going to make it back to heaven by forcing and insistency, and by continually churning over and over again that original 1948 experience, so I just started crying on the train in Japan—realizing I wasn't going to get to heaven. And the minute I began crying, I found myself in Heaven again, very briefly. So there's a poem called *The Change,* which records that. That's just one more poignant moment in disillusionment, of the slow process of getting the visionary monkey off my back. The remarkable thing is that I stupefied myself from 1948 to about 1963. A long time—that's fifteen years, preoccupied with one single thought.

There's some early poems that recorded different early takes on this kind of experience. I immediately saw poetry as a hermetic or secret way of talking about experiences that were universal, cosmic, that everybody knew about, but nobody knew how to talk about, nobody knew how to refer to. Nobody knew how to bring it up to front brain consciousness or to present it to social consciousness. So there were these poems from 1948 and after, where I first found myself a poet with something to talk about. Thus *Vision 1948*: "I shudder with intelligence and I / Wake in the deep light / And hear a vast machinery / Descending without sound, / Intolerable to me, too bright . . ."[8] That was a description of the last experience of terror, a fear that the universe was turning inside out. In *Refrain*[9] a month later, I was beginning to realize I was getting hung up on my visions. "Shadow changes into bone" was my symbolic language, slogan, meaning that Thought (high intellectual thought, ambition, idealized desire) actually comes true, and you do get to see a vision of eternity, which kills you. So "shadow," mind insight, changes into three dimensional "bone."

I had just been in the middle of a broken-up love affair with Neal Cassady which had come to an end at the moment, I thought, and I was desolate. And so, combining the end of the love affair and the visionary experience, I wrote a song called *A Western Ballad,* that was influenced a lot by Blake's rhymes. "I wearied in an endless maze / that men have walked for centuries"[10] is a paraphrase of Blake's *The Voice of the Ancient Bard*: "They stumble all night over the bones of the dead / And wish to lead others when they should be led."

P.P.: Was music part of the poem (*A Western Ballad*) when you wrote it in 1948?

A.G.: No, I put that in—maybe twenty years later. Actually, I'd heard it in inner ear, it was actually there, but at the time, I didn't have an instrument, I didn't play music: but it was built into the rhythm and tones of the poem. The exact notes, probably not, but (sings) "I ain't got no use for the women / A true one can never be found / They'll stick with a man when he's winning, / And laugh in his face when he's down. / My friend was an honest cowpuncher, / Honest and upright and true, / And he'd still be a-ridin' the ranges, / If it weren't for a gal named Lou. / He fell in with evil companions / The kind that were better off dead / And I couldn't help think of that woman / when they filled him full of lead . . ."[*Laughs.*] That was the only "western ballad" I knew how to sing around that time.

Blake's advice on that subject of how you deal with the terror was: "To find the Western Path, / Right thro' the Gates of Wrath / I urge my way . . ."[11] Well, I thought that Blake's instructions meant delve right into the terror, cultivate the terror, get right into it, right into death. I said, "Die, go mad, drop dead." So I thought for many years that my obligation was to annihilate my ordinary consciousness and expand my mystic consciousness through death, I thought "the path" was through the Gates of Wrath; Fear, and Wrath, and Terror. So actually for that fifteen years, I was in a kind of quandary.

P.P.: Are there specific poems that work with that problem?

A.G.: So my first prayer—I got into looking at things in terms of I'd better beg for mercy or something, "Ah still Lord, ah, sweet Divinity . . ." By the time of this "Psalm" a year later (1949),[12] the actual experience had become solidified into the symbol of a god, the notion of a central divine Lord that I was trying to get to. Thus after a while, I wrote big masochistic psalms of the divinity, saying I want to die and be part of You. Which is a classic poetic position a lot of people get trapped into and finally die, too. Thinking well, I'm going to pursue the beauty to the tomb. Saying the body has to drop down the body has to die, and the mind has to die: "When I think of death / I get a goofy feeling: / Then I catch my breath: / Zero is appealing / Appearances are hazy. / Smart went crazy, / Smart went crazy."[13] Christopher Smart. Then Kerouac and I collaborated on a really mad ditty, referring still to the subject of "frantic light"—the basic idea was that only by being torn apart, dying or being cracked open, or going nuts or making

a breakthrough or being turned upside down or inside out
or ass by mouth or finally sort of mind suicided, would there
be any breakthrough opening: "Pull my daisy / Tip my
cup / All my doors are open."[14]

P.P.: Your interpretation of the vision changed as time
passed?

A.G.: Yeah, by 1950, I was already sufficiently disillusioned
to be hip to the fact that I was stuck on a broken record,
mentally. So there are a couple of sort of self-pitying poems,
in a way, saying good-bye to the whole experience, like *An
Imaginary Rose in a Book*.[15] See, by this time I was seeing
the experience as failed, passed, imaginary or hallucinatory,
began to be *willing* to see it as that. "Oh dry old rose of
God . . ." (Ah, *The Sick Rose*, O Rose thou art sick . . .)
"that with such bleak perfume / changed images to blood
. . ."—changed poetry to reality, changed, you know, prophetic mind thoughts to three dimensional, stuck-in-the-
universe actuality. I just finally had to cut that whole set
of thoughts out. By 1951, *Ode: My 24th Year* is all done in
like symbolic language, but I was thinking in terms of
getting grounded again: "Time gets thicker, light gets
dim. . . ."[16] Borne into my body again, "the weaving of the
shroud goes on." I was faced with an actual death rather
than an imaginary spiritual death. Actually, I just gave up,
about that time, age twenty-five, having gone through a
whole cycle of inspiration and dead end. A lot of people go
through that traditional characteristic cycle.

P.P.: So trying to conjure Blake symbolically was a dead
end? What happened after that whole phase of abstraction
and metaphysics?

A.G.: The next stage was a funny compromise. Thinking
that, OK, I can't make it by juggling symbolic language,
referring to roses, light, spiritual wars, ineffable visions—so
the only thing I can do is attempt to describe what I actually
see, or actually saw, to pay attention to detail. To pay attention to minute particulars—so that I could have my cake *and*
eat it, in a way. Like look out at the world as if I were having a vision and see the sort of details I might observe if I

were having a vision. Maybe not look for the entire vision, but at least check out little details like the particular pale greeniness of the buds on the south end of the tips of branches of the trees in the backyard where they're pointing at the sun. The pale budgreen budding of the new bud, as distinct from the older, thick, dark green of the regular leaves. So, noticing detail. Around that time, 1949 on, I ran into William Carlos Williams. Naturally the same thought came to me—was Williams living, actually living, in eternity? observing the detail of eternity, refusing to point to it as eternity, refusing to talk about it in "poetic" terms, refusing to talk about it symbolically—but just directly perceiving what was in front of him? And I realized that's what Blake also said to do, Blake said poetry's in "Minute Particulars." And Williams said No ideas (about eternity!) . . . "No ideas but in things themselves . . . No ideas, but in the facts." So I began accidentally picking up on Williams' work because he lived near me, I began writing poems that were an imitation of his style, which were little short notations of detail. That book, called *Empty Mirror*, I wrote about the same time as *Gates of Wrath*. I'd sent a bunch of these poems (from *Gates*) to Williams, and he wrote back that they weren't very good. What he said was, "In this mode, perfection is basic," these are imperfect. I understood that to mean that there was very little actual concrete detail in them, it was all a sort of refining of the imagery of roses and light and mystical references—rehashing of it over again. I'd thought maybe if I could concentrate all my mind's focus into these few symbols and juggle them around a couple of times—you know, make some crystal-like perfect symbolic statement that would turn other people on and catalyze the same vision in them. But it didn't work, it didn't seem to work. So what I did was to turn to prose so to speak, to little prosaic observations. In Buddhist terms this would be Vipashyana, i.e. paying attention to mindful detail, a sharpening of focus to a finer clearer zennish perception of a black scrape on the floor where a chair has been pulled away; that one detail indicat-

ing a whole path of previous activity. Seeing what's in front
of the eyes, seeing where the eye strikes. Or, "sight is where
the eye hits," a phrase of Louis Zukofsky. The action in
Empty Mirror was something that I've noticed applicable to
a lot of younger students now: the difficulty they have in
turning their minds aside from an idealized notion of visionary perception or social revolutionary perception that
they're seeking. Turning away from an abstract reference of
that, and settling for presentation of what's "closest to the
nose." Settling for what they can actually see in front of
them as a subject for poems. Settling on something they can
say without humorless exaggeration. I see a lot of poetry,
floods of visionary revolutionary post-beatnik, post-hippie,
post-psychedelic poetry coming across my desk, and the
problem is almost everywhere the same problem that I
had—of using referential language pointing to some other
vision out of mind: or something that has been realized but
the poet is not presently in that state, and is violently demanding a breakthrough into a state of universal
consciousness but is not presenting any *details* from that
state of universal consciousness. So the only strategy to get to
that visionary poesy, to approximate it, is to slow down and
fake it, so to speak—it might be interesting to try and fake
it—by simply settling for whatever detail you could actually
see right now, anytime, with ordinary mind.

So (here in *Empty Mirror*), my comment on my previous
poems was "Seven years' words wasted . . ."[17] [*He reads*
Long Live the Spiderweb.] That was a comment on the
whole *Gates of Wrath*. Further, "I attempted to concentrate
/ the total sun's rays in / each poem as through a glass, / but
such magnification / did not set the page afire."[18] So I had
to move on.

"How sick I am! / that thought / always comes to me /
with horror . . ."[19] See now, here's a shift of diction
and of approach to poetry that's more realistic—I'm still day-
dreaming, still talking about my own thoughts, but at least
talking about it in a normal tone of voice that you can understand. "It is December / almost, they are singing /

Christmas carols / in front of the department / stores down the block on / Fourteenth Street." That was my big break-through, finally; it's called *Marijuana Notation*. It took a little grass to make me realize I had been "ignoring other parts of my mind." In "attempting to magnify the sun's rays in each poem as through a glass,"[20] I'd been ignoring every-day perceptions, the more familiar perceptions. Here, the mind-poem shifts from daydreamy introspection as to the nature of consciousness, directly to: "they are singing / Christmas carols. . . ."[21] I remember this poem as being like a big deal for me, because it was the first time that a real literal physical object from my own world entered into a poem. At this time I had got out of a bughouse and was living on my own—actually, a very good state, aware of the situation and moving toward more realistic approaches to my mindthought. Looking at the worst! "Tonite all is well . . ."[22] At that point, there was a certain humor entering in, about my own situation, and dealing with it a little more observantly—the terrible idea of being so totally freaked out that "my head was separated from my body" seemed all right as long as I could talk about it sensibly!

P.P.: Didn't you write another poem in that same room, the room where in "Tonite all is well . . ." you're lying sleepless on the couch?"

A.G.: Yeah. In the same room, on the same couch, looking out the window. There's a line by Yeats, a title in his essays, called *The Trembling of the Veil*. I took that to mean the trembling of the veil of perception, trembling of the veils of eternity. So I put that title on one sort of homely everyday instance of the trembling of the veil of maya, change of perception, and wrote "Today out of the window / the trees seemed like live / organisms on the moon. . . ."[23] [*He reads* The Trembling of the Veil.] I was just looking out the window, trying to describe (as in *Marijuana Notation*) a little piece of actuality in detail. I intended to fix my mind, to root my mind, ground my mind somewhere—in a common place that other people could see. And I figured that if I was in Eternity, or if I was a poet, or if I was a spiritual angel, or if mind was open, there wasn't anything I could do about it, except maybe look at something specific. And describe that. If other people could see through my eyes, whatever Virtu I had would shiver in their brain. In other words, the only way I could actually communicate the sense of eternity that I had, or might have, or wanted to have, was through concrete particular detail grounding my mind, like taking the opposite direction of the superhuman apocalyptic-light-hunger poetry that I'd been churning out before: taking exactly the opposite direction by turning around to face everyday universe, BE HUMAN! So I wrote a series of real simple poems dealing with that, and also looked over all my old writing to see if I had anything in my poem-journals that was real—that actually did cover day-to-day perceptions.

p.p.: Didn't you send those to Williams—after you arranged the journal entries into verse?

a.g.: Yeah, I found a couple of prose things I'd written and arranged them into "modern poetry" lines and sent them off to Williams. His immediate reaction was "This is it! Do you have any more writings like this?" So among the poems I sent to Williams, which to him seemed to demonstrate a grounded mind or someone who'd finally come down to earth, was *A poem on America.*[24] *Acis and Galatea,* those images are all from Dostoevsky's *Raw Youth,* it was a really terrific book, about this Russian kid who has a vision, just like me. I was still referring to my visionary experiences, "filled with fire / with the appearance of God," but at least I got my mind grounded enough to: "The alleys, the dye works, / Mill St. in the smoke, / negros climbing around / the rusted iron by the river . . ."[25] I think that actually may be the best poetry I ever wrote! Just absolutely pure clear modern—you know, one hundred years from now it'll be like looking down the wrong end of the telescope into the past, and you'll see the present time, looking into the eternity of 1949.

p.p.: Allen, how could you have been writing the abstract poems in *Gates of Wrath* while simultaneously writing prose observations in a clear, detailed style? Wasn't that kind of "schitzy"?

A.G.: It was. It's really interesting: a homely poetic schizophrenia. These were written in notebooks, you know, little journals that a lot of us keep. And I wasn't trying to write poetry. So not trying to write poetry, I wasn't, then, obsessed with writing the eternal-image-symbol combination to break everybody's mind open. I was just describing what was in front of me. Because I was doing that, my notes were less obsessional, less hung up, they were just detail. After I met Williams and understood what he was doing, I separated a couple paragraphs with word-pictures out of my journals and arranged them in lines like him—sometimes counting syllables, sometimes counting breath, sometimes balancing it on the page to see what it looked like—visually. These are just the ordinary, unself-conscious notebooks, prose, and I just took the nuts out of it, the intensest moments of prose, pushing everything else aside, isolating it, framing it on the page. It's like a painter paints a big painting—You know the abstract expressionist era? They paint a big painting, and then there are one or two little spots on the painting that they thought had funny kind of tension and space. They'd white-paint out everything else and leave the reds and the blues in just a few areas. Remember? That's what I did with my journals. I just sort of got rid of everything except a couple of lines that were active. That was Williams' advice. He said better have one active phrase—by "active" he meant alive, focused, precise, grounded, no ideas—things—but not ideas. Better have one active phrase, than pages of inactive opaque poetry—poetry that doesn't move. Better isolate just the one thing that's active. That's what poetry does, some kind of mental action . . . contact with reality, rather than waiting, rather than more babbling vagueness. I just eliminated hundreds of pages of subjective scribbling about when will I see Blake again, or I'm crazy, or when are they going to love me, is blank ever gonna come back, what is the nature of the world, curves of phenomenology . . .

P.P.: Didn't you mention other incidents like the Williams'

one—the other night—that helped change your direction
from abstract to the concrete?

A.G.: Another thing that I did, a big lesson to me, was I
spent several years keeping journals and then left them
months in a friend's apartment on 8th Avenue in New York
in 1947. When I came back I found he'd read through all
my secret journals. I was ashamed, it had all this sex stuff
and love babblings about Cassady, and Blake and everything. So I asked him about it, and he said, "Well, it's awful.
Can't read it, it's unreadable." There was only one page that
was readable. I asked what was that? and he pointed to a
page, the only page of actual description of something outside of my head. So I took that out of my journals and rear-
ranged it as *The Bricklayer's Lunch Hour.* [*He reads* The
Bricklayer's Lunch Hour.[26]] It's just sort of like looking out
of the window—sketching. It was something—actually, I got
it off Kerouac, the idea of making a verbal picture. Like
making a little pencil sketch. Detail a cat, a hat, a tree
moving in the wind, etc. Oddly enough, right now, looking
outside, "it's darkening as if to rain and / The wind on top
of the trees in the streets comes through almost harshly."
Without even intending it, there is that little shiver of a
moment in time preserved in the crystal cabinet of the
mind. A little shiver of eternal space, that's what I was looking for. Simply by looking outside of the window and seeing
what was there. That [The Bricklayer's Lunch Hour] is
probably the earliest text I published which makes real
sense. I wrote it in Denver, in my journal, 1947.

P.P.: So you were settling for a more realized, clearer-de-
tail style?

A.G.: See this entry is earlier than the *Gates of Wrath* even.
This ordinary consciousness was available all along. Except I
despised it and thought it was not important, or didn't avail
myself of my own intelligence, my own direct detailed
perception. This is 1947 and all other symbolic churning
doesn't have the Bricklayer's clarity. Which is better? I don't
know. The other kind, in *Gates of Wrath,* is a kind of
mantric magical onanistic, masturbatory sing-along power.

P.P.: Wasn't there another incident, with Kerouac, I think; you mentioned it the other night. Along the line of convincing you to turn away from the symbolic style . . .

A.G.: Yeah. I think about the best funniest of all poems in *Empty Mirror* is represented as . . . finally I get a look at myself from the outside, like in a movie, a burned-out case, a total flop, failure, that I considered I was. I'd gotten out of the bug house, and thought I'd finally hit the ground and didn't have anything. I had a job in market research, a little furnished room on 15th St. in New York. And I wrote this: *Walking home at night.*[27] [*He reads* "Walking home at night.] "I reached my hands to my head and hissed / Oh, God how horrible!"[28] The taste of actual mind thought, of self thought in that is so accurate—it's just like a little flash picture of oneself in a funny moment. And it's clear and familiar. I showed it to Kerouac, he said: "Allen, you really got it there, it's my own little Allen. That's actually Allen. Whoever you are, you're right there. You know—like unashamed, completely free." He bought it, so to speak, and accepted the worst possible image instead of accepting an image of myself as an angel—accepting myself as a soft, white-fleshed failure . . . "creeping / in and out of rooms like / myself."[29] Stuck drab "God, How horrible!" It was just willingness to be that nowhere man, nowhere self, to be myself, really, and the humor involved in being that— rather than being a divine Blakean angel! I think that finally makes it possible to stand firmly on the ground in poems like this and then begin constructing out of that reality; "I saw the best minds of my generation destroyed by madness, starving hysterical naked."[30] Having accepted all that fact, all that detail, and looking at it sympathetically, rather than totally freaked out, working with that ordinary failure; ordinary magic. Then after several years it's possible to build a rhapsody of facts, which is *Howl* a later period.

So, basically what I've done in this talk is cover the development of my poetry up to about 1953, a couple of years before *Howl*. How I was preparing for application of basic grounded realistic humor to the practical world. More free energy for that, once having found a place to put my feet, once having got grounded a little—then getting a little playful maybe, or even have big rhapsodies on the people who've lost their visions.

Does this make sense? Does anybody feel that I took the wrong turn? Made the wrong decision spiritually? Maybe I should have held out for more, got into the bug house and held out for more?

P.P.: Do you ever wish you could go back to 1948, age twenty-two, and start again with the Blake vision?

A.G.: Go back to twenty-two or twenty-three and start all over again? Well, in the tantric Buddhist tradition you do that. It's really miraculous, in a sense, the advent of Buddhism—or if not Buddhism, at least Gnostic experience, the breakthrough (culturally) of the Gnostic tradition because Blake is in that tradition, which is parallel to the Oriental knowledge, mind knowledge. It's a whole new movie! It starts a whole new movie in America where everybody raises his hand and has had a vision. It's really terrific, and what's going to come out of that is something that is going to astound the imaginary angels. Before, maybe people had visions, my theory is that they were just pushed to the back of the brain; they weren't socially usable, they weren't anything you could "work" with. Now you can build a rock band out of visions. Electricians went before you. You could make movies out of it, you could probably build industries on an ecological vision of everything intertwined in nature.

P.P.: Like Solari . . .

A.G.: You could make money on visions, nowadays, you can reform the society. You could reconstitute the nature of the society, or direction. One thing Kerouac said in 1961, that I always took as a keystone, one key statement—when Leary visited and turned everyone on to psylicibin. Kerouac, high, turned around and said to the room, "Walking on water wasn't built in a day." And that's basically the situation in America: that having had a vision, dropping acid in the sixties, or having had a breakthrough in the 1940s, it will take decades and decades—cell by cell—to reconstitute the body of

America, build a new physical body. It will take as long to
"unblow" the old consciousness and recreate a physical
world corresponding to our mental picture; it will take as
long to do *that* as it took to build up this physical monster
building classroom we have here. Obviously, you couldn't
transform this relatively ungainly basement cafeteria into a
metaphysically appropriate arcade filled with green bower
leaves and natural sound systems, without decades of slow,
delicate adjustment of the material world to our desire.
Well, this very Naropa school conception, or the notion of a
Kerouac School of Disembodied Poetics, is something that
would have required breakthrough, spiritual breakthrough,
freak-out, into groundedness—beginning at the beginning
putting our worlds together, slowly. "Walking on water
wasn't built in a day," that was the meaning of that.

Q: Why the "Disembodied" poetics, if the emphasis is getting back into the body?

A.G.: That's a joke. Because he's dead, Kerouac's dead, so
he's disembodied so to speak. Also because we were fools
and didn't know what we were getting into. We didn't realize it would be such a serious body. Also because of beatnik
poetic inspiration that made it sound funny. I objected for a
while, saying wait a minute, this is contrary to all the basic
principles enunciated by Pound and Williams and the
imagist, but Trungpa said, Ah, it's pretty funny, why don't
you use it—it's too late to change it. Too late!

P.P.: Before we finish, could you tell the story about Kerouac's reaction to your visions?

A.G.: When I had my Harlem experiences, he was quite
matured, already written *The Town and The City,* or was
preparing his first book. He I think had not yet had quite
that prophetic shudder of sixties' transcendental freak-out
mind so characteristic—I don't think he'd had a totally
"visionary" experience. Mortal human transitoriness was
built into his nature, and into his early prose, but I didn't
think he'd had a full scale breakthrough at the time. I wrote
him a long mysterious letter, not quite referring . . . telling him that something big had happened to my mind, that

I had entered the kingdom of eternity, that I would come through and teach him as soon as I could. He read it, and it looked to him as if I had really gone nuts. "Poor little Allen, he's really, wants to make something, you know he's going to come and teach me about eternity? Poor little kid." Except that he *was* struck by this sudden seizure of Un-New Jerseyesque, middle-class Jewish-boy-seriousness on my part, that I had suddenly gotten to be a fanatic of some kind. Instead of a nice little boy from Paterson, who was always wandering around saying: "Discretion is the better part of valor." All of a sudden, I was dreaming about angels. He sent me a funnier letter than I sent him, saying something like "America is a permissible dream, providing you remember that ants have Americas." Or eternity is a permissible dream, providing that you remember that ants have eternities, little eternities are had by baby mules in musty fields. Actually, that's not what he said; it's another poem.[31] I recorded this emotional transaction in a poem *The Lion for Real*.[32] The lion is symbolic of that Blake vision, each stanza covers like a different attempt on my part to communicate to the professor, to Kerouac, to my family, to my psychiatrist.

However, a couple of years later, Kerouac had a similar situation of isolation, and was sitting in a field in North Carolina in his sister's backyard doing a little yoga breathing he'd learned. He describes the seizure he had suddenly, in which his eyes closed and everything turned to gold, and he fainted and fell back, and saw everything in the universe as "golden ash." That's described in a text called *The Scripture of the Golden Eternity*. I thought I recognized that he'd had some kind of spiritual breakthrough, or incident, or visionary experience, and from then on, we knew what we were talking about back and forth, we began to correlate our mysterious "X" consciousness . . .[33]

Notes

1. See *Paris Review Interviews,* 2nd Series, Edited by George Plimpton.

2. Allen Ginsberg, *Gates of Wrath* (Bolinas, Ca.: Grey Fox Press, 1972) , p. 4.

3. Ibid., p. 9.

4. E.A. Robinson's "Eros Tyrannos."

5. Ginsberg, *Gates of Wrath,* p. 4.

6. Ibid., p. 4.

7a. Ginsberg, *Howl* (San Francisco: City Lights, 1956) , p. 41.

7. Ibid., p. 15.

8. Ginsberg, *Gates of Wrath,* p. 7.

9. Ibid., p. 10.

10. Ibid., p. 11

11. Poems from the *Rossetti Manuscript,* by William Blake.

12. Ginsberg, *Gates of Wrath,* p. 16.

13. Ibid., p. 24.

14. Ibid., p. 27, 28.

15. Ibid., p. 37.

16. Ibid., p. 40.

17. Ginsberg, *Empty Mirror* (New York: Totem/Corinth, 1970) , p. 22.

18. Ibid., p. 23.

19. Ibid., p. 24.

20. Paraphrase of poem "I attempted to concentrate . . . ," from *Empty Mirror.*

21. Ibid., p. 25.

22. Ibid., p. 10.

23. Ibid., p. 15.

24. Ibid., p. 40.

25. Ibid.

26. Ibid., p. 41.

27. Ibid., p. 59.

28. Ibid.

29. Ibid.

30. Ginsberg, *Howl,* p. 9.

31. Jack Kerouac, *Mexico City Blues* (New York: Grove Press, 1959) , p. 51.

32. Ginsberg, *Kaddish* (San Francisco: City Lights, 1961), p. 53-55.

33. Gregory Corso, from *Hydra,* late 50s. Wrote on an experience of "Skinless Light."

GENERAL PRACTICE OF THE JACK KEROUAC SCHOOL OF DISEMBODIED POETICS AT NAROPA INSTITUTE

THURSDAY

I have had my dream—like others—
and it has come to nothing, so that
I remain now carelessly
with feet planted on the ground
and look up at the sky—
feeling my clothes about me,
the weight of my body in my shoes,
the rim of my hat, air passing in and out
at my nose—and decide to dream no more.

—William Carlos Williams

OBSERVING AN INTERPENETRATION of Eastern and Western human arts, the Poetics Program at Naropa Institute combines study of traditional Western poetic composition up to present century (with special emphasis on writing creation that reflects mind nature observed during composition time), with traditional Eastern meditation discipline, commonly sitting following breath. In primarily Buddhist atmosphere, where classical meditation provides common spirit approach in study of psychology, dance, theater, music, painting, and Buddhist mind, the Poetics program was worked out:

1) To link Western traditions of spontaneous composition with oriental practice of the same—historically represented by the lineages of Milarepa the poet, Japanese zen haiku and the poetic sayings and writings of Indian, Chinese and other spiritual poets.

2) To reinforce the basic concerns of Naropa Institute in context of creative writing by grounding the student in practical observation of .detail, attention to concrete particulars and a sane relationship to the phenomenal world.

3) To influence both poetry teachers and students in the direction of classical meditation practices, and to influence the Naropa meditative community in the direction of practical poetic articulation of their personal experience.

Meditators' mouths are shaped to address the large American ear with clear voice on their discoveries in subjective space: U.S. poets are encouraged to hallow their voices to include depths of silent observation usually associated with classical meditative psyche. Intersection point of these two traditions occurs during development and refinement of spontaneous-mind poetic activity for purposes of teaching, enlightenment and beauty, or aesthetic pleasure.

4) To honor poetry itself: teaching in the Poetics Program is done by practicing poets whose primary preoccupation heretofore has been poeticizing rather than teaching, and who have become committed to the Naropa Program through a unique circumstance offering open space for active bards to teach specialized students. We propose to inspire actual creative writing with a background of meditation beneath the academic office. Creative writing itself is seen as awareness "practice." Our main concern is to create poetry, complemented by criticism or scholarship, as an end in itself as well as a vehicle for background Buddhistic studies, or studies of the mind's realities.

5) To join the energy of postwar, modern, hip, non-linear new poetry practice, sometimes considered undisciplined, with the older disciplined traditions of contemplative activity: to unite native American poetic freedoms and perceptions with an international tradition of spiritual liberation that has survived millenia while developing an ongoing body of aware experience.

6) To develop and explore existing texts as a conscious probe (attitude toward writing as a probe) into different imaginative energies of life and death, utilizing ancient and modern literary methods and practices: collage, cut-up, dream and journal investigations, spontaneous composition, chance operation, social investigative scholarship, song, classical quantitative prosody study, found-object aesthetics, confession & narrative, all of which encourage playful awareness that transforms everyday work to art.

7) To continue a tradition of national convocation of American poets working with open form (specifically active figures in so-called San Francisco Renaissance, New York and Black Mountain Schools, beat and projective movements, and Tulsa White Dovest, among others) which cohered in Vancouver, 1963 and continued in the Berkeley Poetry Conference, 1965. Many participants in these now historic conferences have taught as members or core faculty of the Kerouac School of Disembodied Poetics at Naropa since summer 1974. The Visiting Poetics Academy consists in weekly series of lectures and poetry readings by celebrated poet visitors; workshop courses; student-faculty readings; tape and book library; faculty-student publications (*Loka,* published by Doubleday in New York, Vols. I & II, *Sitting Frog,* published in Maine, 1975, *Bombay Gin* and *Attaboy,* published in Boulder, 1975, 1976, 1977, and *Roof,* published in New York, 1976) ; transmission of lectures as local, Pacifica, and other radio broadcasts; videotapes; special conferences on poetics; resident poets, such as William Burroughs and Gregory Corso, teaching and sharing the session or summer; many transient poets arriving, teaching, depart-

ing; and active Kerouac school intercourse with the local
(Boulder-Denver) poetic community.

The following poets have taught at Naropa since 1974:
Core Faculty: Anne Waldman, Allen Ginsberg, Dick Gal-
lup, Michael Brownstein. Long Residence: William Bur-
roughs, Gregory Corso, Diane di Prima, Philip Whalen,
Larry Fagin, Peter Orlovsky, Ed Sanders, Michael McClure,
Joanne Kyger, Robert Duncan, and Tom Veitch. Visiting
Poets: John Ashbery, Ted Berrigan, Ron Padgett, Sidney
Goldfarb, John Giorno, Jerome Rothenberg, Diane Wakoski,
Robert Creeley, Amiri Baraka, Kate Millett, Ken Kesey,
Miguel Algarin, Alice Notley, Bernadette Mayer, Lewis
Warsh, Kenward Elmslie, Jackson Mac Low, Helen Adam,
George Quasha, John Cage, Jack Collom, Bobbie Louise
Hawkins, and others.

8) Though not all the poetry teachers are Buddhist, nor
is it required of the teachers and students in this secular
school to follow any specific meditative path, it is the happy
accident of this century's poetic history—especially since Gertrude Stein—that the quality of mind and mindfulness
probed by U.S. poetry is related to quality of mind probed
by Buddhist practice. There being no party line but
mindfulness of thought and language itself, no conflict need
rise between "religion" and "poetry," and the marriage of
two disciplines at Naropa has survived four years and is expected to flourish during the next hundred.

ADDENDUM: TEACHING STRATEGIES

As suggested, where students and teachers share common
ground of silent meditation practice, there is advantage of
shared experience of mind-functioning, which serves as some
basis of study of articulation of mind, here seen as poetics.

Thanks to school smallness and intimacy of activities, as
well as common purpose between teacher & students—
namely creating poetry out of mind study—there's the
possibility of informal social mingling & continuous

student-teacher & interdisciplinary interchange; these basic circumstances, historically, encourage poetic communities. Poets collaborate with dancers, classic folk and dance musicians, theater bands, physicists, psychologists, ecologists, & Zen Masters. Since most of the poets are renowned or poet's-poet renowned Bards, it's possible to work with older-fashioned set-up of apprentices, i.e., students actually helping teachers get together their own work, editing and typing and preparing for publication various manuscripts & collections of writings by poetry masters. Similar to earlier Indo-European traditions in painting and philosophy, this discipline-apprentice tradition has figured in both literature of the West & meditation studies of the East.

Network of companion-poets several decades old continues to be assembled—for the Visiting Poetics Academy —to involve the students in the creation of the poetic community, an age-old relation here transposed for this rare occasion into academic situation—i.e. classicists, orientalists, older gay poetry gangs, beat poetry gangs, Tulsa Wichita & SF poetry gangs, NY St. Mark's Poetry Project community, Buddhist West Coast Tendency, Bohemian-liberation schools, Americanist traditionalist agrarian poets, Amerindian specialists, folk pop rock Blues minstrels, Stone Soup Poets, "Newyorican" language men—students and teachers of all these elements familiar and vital to U.S. poetry over last thirty years have been given place, space and functional welcome at Naropa. It is of advantage for students of poetry to come into direct contact with older poets, living members of forementioned "schools." Nor has traditional academic style been neglected or excluded—thus participation by experienced Professor-Scholar poets: Robert Creeley, Jerome Rothenberg, Ted Berrigan, John Ashbery, etc., who have had long experience in professional roles at major American universities, edited historic magazines and compiled many anthologies much studied in Literary Academies.

Poetry readings where students and teachers share stage are part of that strategy necessary to teach vocalization of texts, an important element in the Naropa tradition, style &

practice of poetry: reading aloud, the poem as a spoken action, even as a spontaneously spoken happening.

Poetic practice at Naropa thus includes spontaneous or un-revised utterance of rhymes & images without rhyme that rise naturally as passing thought-forms and breath rhythms during moments of composition. This lore common to oriental & ancient bardic & modern blues Poetics, also draws from experiments in direct transcription of mental grammatical forms by Gertrude Stein.

We poets at Naropa also seek to discern in American speech, by rule of thumb variable foot or breath stop, syllable, vowel or phrase-unit count, some measure for the line of verse, to balance groups of lines, and encourage mindfulness in transcription of written & spontaneous poetics—that the page has intelligible and often beautiful shape, the verses outline the appearance, flowering and dissolution of thought forms, one succeeding another with gaps in between.

The Jack Kerouac School of
Disembodied Poetics

Allen Ginsberg, with
Anne Waldman and
Michael Brownstein

August 1976
Revised July 1978

BIOGRAPHICAL NOTES

MIGUEL ALGARIN was born in 1941 in Puerto Rico and came to the United States in 1950. He was educated at the University of Wisconsin, Pennsylvania State University, and did further graduate study at Rutgers University where he now teaches English. Mr. Algarin is the founder of the Nuyorican Poets' Cafe in New York City and the executive director of the Nuyorican Theater Festival. He has given poetry readings throughout the United States, The Netherlands, and France. He co-authored and edited *Nuyorican Poetry: An Anthology of Puerto Rican Words and Feelings.*

TED BERRIGAN was born in 1934 in Providence, Rhode Island. He received a B.A. and an M.A. from Tulsa University and edited *C* Magazine in New York City in the sixties. His books include *Bean Spasms* (with Ron Padgett and Joe Brainard), *The Sonnets, Many Happy Returns, In the Early Morning Rain, A Feeling for Leaving, Red Wagon* and *Nothing for You.* His only novel is titled *Clear the Range.* He has taught at the Iowa Writers' Workshop, the University of Michigan, the University of Essex in England, Northeastern Illinois University in Chicago and at the Poetry Project at St. Mark's Church-in-the-Bowery in New York City. He participated in the Visiting Poetics Academy at Naropa Institute in the summers of 1975, 1976 and 1978.

MICHAEL BROWNSTEIN was born August 25, 1943 and grew up in rural South Jersey, suburban east Tennessee and Cleveland, Ohio. He attended Antioch College and the New School for Social Research and was a Fulbright Fellow in Paris, France, 1967-1968, translating modern French poetry. He received the Frank O'Hara award for poetry in 1969, resulting in the publication of his first book *Highway to the Sky,* (Columbia University Press, 1969). His other books include *Brainstorms,* a collection of short prose works and fiction (Bobbs-Merrill, 1971) *Country Cousins,* a novel (George Braziller, Inc., 1974); and *Strange Days Ahead,* a book of poetry (Z Press, Calais, Vermont, 1975). He is the assistant director of the Jack Kerouac School of Disembodied Poetics at Naropa Institute and has been on the core faculty at Naropa since 1976.

WILLIAM S. BURROUGHS was born in St. Louis, Missouri on February 5, 1914. He studied at Harvard, traveled around Europe between the wars and worked odd-jobs in New York City in the early forties. He later traveled extensively in North Africa and Europe, living during the fifties and sixties in Tangiers, Paris and London. He returned to the United States in the seventies, and now maintains a loft in the Bowery of New York City, as well as an apartment in Boulder, Colorado. He has taught regularly at Naropa Institute since 1975. His books include *Junky, Naked Lunch, Nova Express, The Soft Machine, The Ticket That Exploded, The Last Words of Dutch Schultz, Exterminator,* and *Cities of The Red Night.*

CLARK COOLIDGE was born in 1939 in Providence, Rhode Island and now lives with his wife Susan and daughter Celia in the Berkshire Hills of western Massachusetts. He has worked as musician (bebop/classical drums), disc jockey, library searcher and cave explorer. He received a Poets' Foundation Award in 1967 and an NEA Grant in 1977. Recent books include *The Maintains, Polaroid* and *Quartz Hearts.*

DIANE DI PRIMA was born in 1934 in New York City. She attended Swarthmore College for a year and a half and then left to concentrate on her own writing. From 1961 to 1963 she was co-editor of *The Floating Bear* with LeRoi Jones (Amiri Baraka), and she continued sole editorship of this mimeographed newsletter of new writing until 1970. She helped found the New York Poets' Theatre in 1961, which produced plays by Robert Duncan, Frank O'Hara, John Wieners, James Schuyler and others, and in 1964 founded the Poets Press in New York, which published twenty-three books of poetry and prose. In 1974 she began to publish books through Eidolon Editions. She has had over twenty volumes of her own poetry published, the most recent being *Selected Poems: 1956-1975* (North Atlantic Books) ; *Travel Poems & Journals,* (Peace Press, 1978) ; and *Loba, in Progress* (Wingbow Press, 1978). In 1968 she moved to San Francisco where she studied Buddhism for four years with Shunryu Suzuki Roshi at Zen Center. She helped establish the Jack Kerouac School of Disembodied Poetics at Naropa Institute in 1974 and has been a member of the Visiting Poetics Academy ever since.

EDWARD DORN was born in the prairie town of Villa Grove, Illinois on April 2, 1929. He attended Black Mountain College and has taught in universities in Idaho, New Mexico, California, Chicago, Colorado and England. His books include *The Newly Fallen, North Atlantic Turbine, Some Business Recently Transacted in the White World, Gunslinger* and *Hello La Jolla.*

ROBERT DUNCAN was born January 7, 1919 in Oakland, California. He edited *Experimental Review* during World War II and his work appeared in *Origins* Magazine in the early fifties. He is the recipient of numerous awards, including the Union League and Arts Foundation Prize in 1957, and the Levinson Prize in 1964, and he received a Guggenheim Fellowship in 1963 and 1964. He is the author of *Heavenly City, Earthly City, Roots and Branches, The Opening of the Field, Caesar's Gate, The First Decade, The Day the Sun Fell, Dante* and others.

JOHN CAGE, the composer, writer and performer, was born in 1912, the son of an inventor in Los Angeles, California. He attended Pomona College, where some rebellious behavior hastened his departure to Europe. There he worked in the fields of architecture, poetry, painting and composing. He later studied with Arnold Schoenberg, and in his early musical career, he earned money by accompanying dancers on the piano. Many of his early piano pieces were composed for his friend and closest professional associate, Merce Cunningham. Mr. Cage was the inventor of the "prepared" piano, first used in his piece "Bacchanale" in 1938. He extended "atonal" music into non-pitched sounds, or "noise," using bolts, screws, glass and rubber as instruments, in pieces such as "The Perilous Night" and "Root of an Unfocus." His single most notorious composition is "The Silent Piece," officially titled *4'33".* His two books *Silence* (1961) and *A Year from Monday* (1967) are underground classics. In recent years he has performed his "word" work at the Poetry Project at St. Mark's Church-in-the-Bowery in New York. He is a member of the National Institute of Arts and Letters.

ALLEN GINSBERG was born June 3, 1926 in Paterson, New Jersey and attended school at Columbia College. He has traveled as a

Merchant Marine, lived in Texas and Denver, worked as a dish-washer, copyboy and a market researcher. He wrote *Howl* in 1955 in San Francisco and *Kaddish* in 1959 in New York City. He lived and traveled in the Orient in the sixties and since then has more or less settled on New York City's Lower East Side, when he is not in residence at the Kerouac School in Boulder which he helped found and has co-directed since 1974. Recent books include *The Fall of America,* which won a National Book Award; *First Blues* (Full Court Press, 1975) ; and *Mind, Breath & Body* (City Lights, 1978). He has been exploring the poetics of meditation and also pop music. Mr. Ginsberg is a member of the National Institute of Arts and Letters.

JACKSON MAC LOW was born September 12, 1922, grew up in Chicago and Kenilworth, Illinois and lived in New York City af-ter 1943. He was a *Cum Laude* Greek major at Brooklyn College, 1958 and wrote music for the Living Theatre's production of W.H. Auden's *Age of Anxiety,* 1954. He has had musical compositions performed in America, France, Italy, Ger-many and Denmark, and has been active in pacifist and anar-chist movements since the 1940s. His books include *Stanzas for Iris Lezak,* Else Press, 1972. He is an active "word" performer and often conducts orchestras of other voices.

Mr. Mac Low says of himself:

> I thought it more important to provide a background centering on my own art and that of Cage, Wolff, Brown, Feldman, et. al., & showing some of the links (via Zen) with Dharma, & to show the equally (to my mind) important links between the social situations during performances of simultaneities & those favored/envisaged by anarchists & other libertarians. (That I shd also find meaningful concepts & symbols from the authoritarian Roman Church shd not surprise a student of the monarchic Vajrayana) .
>
> The fact is that John Cage's anarchism has only come out of the closet relatively recently, altho he's been closely asso-ciated with anarchist friends & projects since Black Mountain. The Gate Hill Co-op in Stony Point-Haverstraw NY was founded by John, along with anarchist friends from Black Mountain: Vera & Paul Williams, who sparked the

Co-op project by lending capital & designing & building houses & workshops like the Pottery. Vera was, along with me & David Wieck, the editorial staff of the anarchist magazine *Resistance* during its last few years (1951-54) —she did most of our covers, as she did later for *Liberation*. John's house there was an extension of the Williams' house, separated only by a stone wall which John built himself from field stones. When he came to need more room, Paul designed another part that extended beyond the original room & kitchen. I think I largely got to know John thru the Williamses: I'd met Vera the one day I was at Black Mountain College in summer 1950 visiting the Goodmans, who were teaching there then—I was directing dramatics & drama at Vera Lachmann's Camp Catawba for Boys at Blowing Rock, NC, 100 miles or so north of Black Mountain. Later I again met the Williamses at the Goodmans' in New York, & as the Co-op came into being, I came to spend more & more time there in the middle 50's. I'd met Cage in NY earlier thru another BC friend, & it was thru our casual conversations in the farmhouse & in the woods, &c. at Stony Pt. that I came to be interested in the possibilities offered by aleatoric methods, &c.

So Anarchism, Zen, & modern aleatoric/indeterministic art have had links from the beginning (David Tudor & M. C. Richards were also among the founders of the Gate Hill Co-op—David still lives there, & he and M.C. were among the Black Mountain group that did the 1st happening with John & Bob & others—& Paul Goodman's influence was quite strong on both the Williamses & M.C., who was a very close friend of his at BC. So much for background history.

The main Buddhist influence on all of this was probably Dr. D. T. Suzuki, who was teaching weekly seminars in Zen and Kegon Buddhism at Columbia (c. 1953?-1959), which cd be taken as credit courses in the School of Religion, but which—thru a special arrangement made possible by the Buddhist (presumably) plumbing millionaire Crane—were open gratis to all interested persons. Both John & I as well as other Buddhist artists and students, attended Suzuki's classes with varying regularity. We also read Dr. S's books on Zen & other schools. I don't know & often wonder what Dr. Suzuki wdve made of the art we derived (!) from Zen!

I don't want to sound too pious about all this. The whole history of modern art since John began using I Ching chance operations c. 1950 attests to the fact that Buddhist art needn't be solemn—that Dharma's embodied in concrete experiences of living bodies.

LEWIS MACADAMS was born October 12, 1944 in west Texas. He was raised in Dallas and attended school at both Princeton and S.U.N.Y. in Buffalo. His books include *City Money, The Poetry Room, News from Neiman Farm* and *Dance*. Mr. MacAdams is currently director of the poetry program at San Francisco State University, and he makes his home in Bolinas, California.

MICHAEL MCCLURE was born in the Midwest in 1932 and has attended schools in the Midwest, the Southwest and in San Francisco. He is the author of *Jaguar Skies, Ghost Tantras, Antechamber* and other volumes of poetry. He is also known as a playwright, especially since the first performances of his play, *The Beard,* and has published novels and a book of essays. His major interest outside of poetry is biology.

RON PADGETT was born in Tulsa, Oklahoma in 1942. He has lived for the most part in New York City since 1960. Among his published works are *Great Balls of Fire* (poems), *Bean Spasms* (collaborations with Ted Berrigan), *Antlers in the Treetops* (a novel with Tom Veitch) and most recently *Toujours L'Amour* (poems). He and David Shapiro edited *An Anthology of New York Poets.* He has translated Apollinaire, Duchamp and Cendrars, as well as Valery Larbaud's *The Poems of A.O. Barnabooth* (with Bill Zavatsky). With Anne Waldman and Joan Simon he founded the Full Court Press. Since 1968 he has earned a living teaching poetry in the schools with groups such as Teachers & Writers Collaborative in New York. Recently, he spent two years on a "Writer in the Community" grant in a small textile mill town in South Carolina. He is currently director in residence of the Poetry Project at St. Mark's Church-in-the-Bowery in New York City, where he lives with his wife and son.

JEROME ROTHENBERG was born in New York City in 1931. He came into his own (as poet, editor, translator, stand-up performer, etc.) in the late 1950s, and since then has authored about thirty books of poetry and poetics, plus a number of theatrical, musical and intermedia events. These include *Poland/1931, Poems for the Game of Silence,* and *A Seneca Journal;* the anthologies: *Technicians of the Sacred, Shaking the Pumpkin, America a Prophecy* (with George Quasha), *Revolution of the Word,* and *A Big Jewish Book;* and *Six Horse Songs for Four Voices* ("total translation" from the Navajo). While concerned with the new and experimental, he has described much of his work as "an ongoing attempt to reinterpret the poetic past from the point of view of the present." This has involved him in a series of strategies to which he has given names, such as "deep image," "ethnopoetics" and "total translation," and has it involved him in a series of publishing projects to promote these strategies: *Poems from the Floating World* (Hawk's Well Press) ; *some/thing,* with David Antin; *Alcheringa,* with Dennis Tedlock; and, most recently, *New Wilderness Letter.*

ED SANDERS, poet, novelist, private investigator, is the author of many books including *The Family, Tales of Beatnik Glory, 20,000 A.D.,* and the newly released *Investigative Poetry.* Editor and publisher during the 1960s of the seminal underground magazine *Fuck You: A Magazine of the Arts,* he also was lead singer for the Fugs and remains the only American performer to sing *Swinburne* while touring on the road.

ANNE WALDMAN, born April 2, 1945, grew up on Macdougal Street in New York City. She is the author of seven books of poetry, including *Baby Breakdown, Fast Speaking Woman, Journals & Dreams* and *Shaman;* editor of two anthologies for Bobbs-Merrill; and was assistant and then director of the Poetry Project at St. Mark's Church-in-the-Bowery from 1966 to 1977. She co-founded *Angel Hair* Magazine and Books at the Berkeley Poetry Conference in 1965 and is editor of one of the oldest extant mimeographed magazines, *The World,* now in its thirty-first year of issue. She is also an editor of Full Court Press. She has given numerous poetry readings across the United States and in Europe and has a recording with Giorno Poetry Systems. She was a founder and has been the co-director of the Jack Kerouac School of Disembodied Poetics since 1974. She is a student of Chatral Saugye Dorje, Rinpoche.

PHILIP WHALEN was born in Portland, Oregon on October 20, 1923. He served in the United States Army Air Force and graduated from Reed College with a B.A. in 1951. He is the author of many collections of poetry, including *On Bear's Head, Scenes of Life at the Capital, Severance Pay,* and *The Kindness of Strangers,* and two novels, *You Didn't Even Try* and *Imaginary Speeches for a Brazen Head.* He spent several years living and teaching English in Kyoto, Japan, and in 1972 he began formal Zen study and practice with Richard Baker Roshi at the San Francisco Zen Center and at Zenshinji Monastery, Tassajara Springs. He was ordained a Buddhist monk in 1973. He has taught regularly for the Visiting Poetics Academy at Naropa Institute since 1975.

MARILYN WEBB was born in Brooklyn on October 26, 1942 and has lived at various times in Boston, Chicago, Washington D.C., Vermont, Havana and Paris. She is a journalist who has written for *Ramparts, Redbook* and *MS* magazines, the *Village Voice, East-West Journal, Denver* Magazine and *The Guardian,* among others, and was the recipient of a 1977 National Media Award in Magazine Writing from the American Psychological Association. Pieces of hers have been included in the following books: *And Jill Came Tumbling After,* by Judith Stacey; *The Movement,* by Mitchell Goodman; *Roles Women Play,* by Michelle Garskoff; *Resurrection Theater,* by Marc Estrin; *The New Women,* by Bunche, Weeks, Cooke and Morgan and *Feminist Education,* by Bunche. She taught writing at Goddard College and currently is a reporter for a newspaper in Boulder.